T0212112

Lecture Notes in Computer Science

Lecture Notes in Artificial Intelligence   **14523**

Founding Editor

Jörg Siekmann

Series Editors

Randy Goebel, *University of Alberta, Edmonton, Canada*
Wolfgang Wahlster, *DFKI, Berlin, Germany*
Zhi-Hua Zhou, *Nanjing University, Nanjing, China*

The series Lecture Notes in Artificial Intelligence (LNAI) was established in 1988 as a topical subseries of LNCS devoted to artificial intelligence.

The series publishes state-of-the-art research results at a high level. As with the LNCS mother series, the mission of the series is to serve the international R & D community by providing an invaluable service, mainly focused on the publication of conference and workshop proceedings and postproceedings.

Fabio Cuzzolin · Maryam Sultana
Editors

Epistemic Uncertainty in Artificial Intelligence

First International Workshop, Epi UAI 2023
Pittsburgh, PA, USA, August 4, 2023
Revised Selected Papers

 Springer

Editors
Fabio Cuzzolin 🆔
Oxford Brookes University
Oxford, UK

Maryam Sultana 🆔
Oxford Brookes University
Oxford, UK

ISSN 0302-9743   ISSN 1611-3349 (electronic)
Lecture Notes in Artificial Intelligence
ISBN 978-3-031-57962-2   ISBN 978-3-031-57963-9 (eBook)
https://doi.org/10.1007/978-3-031-57963-9

LNCS Sublibrary: SL7 – Artificial Intelligence

This Springer imprint is published by the registered company Springer Nature Switzerland AG
The registered company address is: Gewerbestrasse 11, 6330 Cham, Switzerland

Paper in this product is recyclable.

Preface

This volume collects the papers presented at the *Epistemic Uncertainty in Artificial Intelligence* (Epi UAI 2023) workshop held at Carnegie Mellon University in Pittsburgh, Pennsylvania, USA on August 4th, 2023 (https://sites.google.com/view/epi-workshop-uai-2023/). The workshop was organized in connection with the project *Epistemic AI* https://www.epistemic-ai.eu/. The project, which has received funding from the European Union's Horizon 2020 research and innovation program under grant agreement No. 964505 (Epi), aims to devise a new paradigm for next-generation artificial intelligence providing worst-case guarantees on its predictions, thanks to proper modeling of real-world uncertainties. This involves formulating a new mathematical framework for constrained optimization under epistemic uncertainty, superseding existing probabilistic approaches, and laying the foundations for the creation of new 'epistemic' learning paradigms. Epistemic AI focuses, in particular, on some of the most important areas of machine learning: unsupervised learning, supervised learning, and reinforcement learning.

As part of this effort, we organized the Epi UAI 2023 workshop to raise awareness around the modeling of epistemic uncertainty in artificial intelligence and machine learning, a rapidly emerging topic in these two communities. As the purpose was to aim for the broadest possible involvement, we as organizers along with program chairs invited the submission of peer-reviewed papers covering a number of topics relevant to uncertainty quantification: Model uncertainty estimation, Robustness to distribution shift, Out-of-distribution generalization, Model adaptation, Datasets and protocols for evaluating uncertainty and robustness, Conformal prediction, Distribution-free uncertainty quantification,Optimization under uncertainty, Uncertainty estimation using deep ensembles, Bayesian deep learning (including approximate inference and Bayesian deep reinforcement learning), Deep recognition models for variational inference, Epistemic learning, Uncertainty in real-world applications (e.g. autonomous driving,healthcare, language models). The recorded version of the entire workshop can be found following this link: (https://youtu.be/rWrvsePXZ9I?si=ha_orKXUQSJW9ROR/). The workshop was held in conjunction with the conference *Uncertainty in Artificial Intelligence* (UAI) whose program included industry exhibitions, demonstrations, and other social events.

Role of Workshop Organizers: The organizing committee for the workshop handled the planning, execution, and coordination. We developed the workshop proposal with the program chairs, and we invited the speakers and secured sponsors.

We received a total of seventeen full papers for review. Following a comprehensive evaluation process by the program chairs and program committee members, sixteen papers were selected for presentation. Unfortunately, one submission was found to be unrelated to the workshop theme and was subsequently desk-rejected. From the original sixteen submissions, eight full papers were ultimately chosen for inclusion in these proceedings. The selection process adhered to a double-blind peer review system, with each submission undergoing an average of two reviews. Reviewers meticulously assessed the papers across various criteria, including originality, significance of the research contribution, technical soundness, clarity of presentation, and alignment with the workshop's theme. Insightful feedback and scores from PC members and reviewers were provided for each paper. The Epi UAI 2023 event spanned a whole day and was articulated into two spotlight/oral sessions and two poster sessions, as well as four keynote lectures by world-class experts in AI and uncertainty quantification. All the keynote speakers have done foundational work on epistemic uncertainty and its machine learning implications.

Gert de Cooman from Ghent University works on developing models for the representation and manipulation of uncertainty, using the behavioral theory of imprecise probabilities. At the workshop, he delivered a keynote session addressing the intriguing topic of 'Imprecision: Why It Is Useful?'. Yarin Gal from Oxford University has made significant contributions to Bayesian deep learning, and approximate Bayesian inference and also works on modeling uncertainty in real-world applications. His enlightening talk centered around 'Foundation Models That Can Tell Us When They Don't Know'. Marco Zaffalon is a renowned expert in imprecise probability (IP) techniques such as credal classifiers in machine learning. His keynote session delved into the intriguing topic of 'Causal Inference Meets Epistemic AI: Practical, General Methods for Counterfactuals and Information Fusion'. Aaditya Ramdas' main research interests include selective and simultaneous inference, game-theoretic statistics, and distribution-free black-box predictive inference. He shared profound insights in his keynote session titled 'Distribution-Free Uncertainty Quantification Under Distribution Drifts and Shifts'.

Accepted papers were presented as either oral or posters, based on the reviewers' comments. We granted spotlight talks to selected top papers. We also presented a Best Paper award with title 'Joint Modelling for Uncertainty Quantification' and a Best Student Paper award with title 'URL: A Representation Learning Benchmark for Transferable Uncertainty Estimates'. The awards were issued based on the PC member's reviews. Our event also included: an introduction to the Epistemic AI project by the organizers; invited talks by top researchers in the area, with brief Q&A sessions; oral presentations for both the Best Paper and the Best Student Paper; spotlight talks; two poster sessions (a morning session and an afternoon session). We concluded the day with a discussion panel on the future of research in uncertainty-aware machine learning.

Although the workshop was funded by the budget of the Epi project, we were also able to secure additional support to fund prizes, speakers travel, and subsistence from outside sponsors. Our academic sponsors included Oxford Brookes University, KU Leuven, TU Delft, and Kyungpook National University in South Korea.

The Epi UAI 2023 Organizing Committee and Program Chairs would like to thank all the authors, the reviewers, and the workshop sponsors for their support.

August 2023

Fabio Cuzzolin
Maryam Sultana
Matthijs Spaan
Keivan Shariatmadar
Kaizheng Wang
Shireen Kudukkil Manchingal

Organization

Workshop Organizers and Editors

Fabio Cuzzolin   Oxford Brookes University, UK
Maryam Sultana   Oxford Brookes University, UK

Program Chairs

Matthijs Spaan   TU Delft, Netherlands
Keivan Shariatmadar   KU Leuven, Belgium
Kaizheng Wang   KU Leuven, Belgium
Shireen Kudukkil Manchingal   Oxford Brookes University, UK

Program Committee

Matthijs Spaan   TU Delft, Netherlands
Keivan Shariatmadar   KU Leuven, Belgium
Kaizheng Wang   KU Leuven, Belgium
Shireen Kudukkil Manchingal   Oxford Brookes University, UK
Andrew Bradley   Oxford Brookes University, UK
Muhammad Mubashar   Oxford Brookes University, UK
Hans Hallez   KU Leuven, Belgium
David Moens   KU Leuven, Belgium
Neil Yorke-Smith   TU Delft, Netherlands
Julian Kooij   TU Delft, Netherlands
Moritz Zanger   TU Delft, Netherlands
Pascal van der Vaart   TU Delft, Netherlands
Noah Schutte   TU Delft, Netherlands
Cassio de Campos   TU Eindhoven, Netherlands
Karthika Mohan   Oregon State University, USA
Naeemullah Khan   KAUST, Kingdom of Saudi Arabia
Gabriele Piergiovanni   Alien Technology Transfer, Italy
Johann Hoffelner   LCM, Austria
Gerrit Timmer   ORTEC, Netherlands

Abstracts

A Novel Bayes' Theorem for Upper Probabilities

Michele Caprio[1], Yusuf Sale[2,3], Eyke Hüllermeier[2,3], and Insup Lee[1]

[1] University of Pennsylvania, Philadelphia, PA, 19104 USA
{caprio,lee}@seas.upenn.edu
[2] University of Munich (LMU), D-80539 Munich, Germany
{yusuf.sale,eyke}@lmu.de
[3] Munich Center for Machine Learning, D-80539 Munich, Germany

Abstract. In their seminal 1990 paper, Wasserman and Kadane establish an upper bound for the Bayes' posterior probability of a measurable set A, when the prior lies in a class of probability measures $\mathcal{P}$ and the likelihood is precise. They also give a sufficient condition for such upper bound to hold with equality. In this paper, we introduce a generalization of their result by additionally addressing uncertainty related to the likelihood. We give an upper bound for the posterior probability when both the prior and the likelihood belong to a set of probabilities. Furthermore, we give a sufficient condition for this upper bound to become an equality. This result is interesting on its own, and has the potential of being applied to various fields of engineering (e.g. model predictive control), machine learning, and artificial intelligence.

Keywords: Probabilistic Machine Learning · Credal Sets · Robust Machine Learning · Imprecise Probabilities · Bayesian inference

Deep Learning and MCMC with aggVAE for Shifting Administrative Boundaries: Mapping Malaria Prevalence in Kenya

Elizaveta Semenova[1,6] , Swapnil Mishra[2,6] , Samir Bhatt[3,4,6] ,
Seth Flaxman[1,6] , and H. Juliette T. Unwin[4,5,6]

[1] Department of Computer Science, University of Oxford, UK
elizaveta.p.semenova@gmail.com, seth.flaxman@cs.ox.ac.uk
[2] Saw Swee Hock School of Public Health and Institute of Data Science, National University
of Singapore and NUHS, Singapore
swapnil.mishra@nus.edu.sg
[3] School of Public Health, University of Copenhagen, Denmark
samir.bhatt@sund.ku.dk
[4] School of Public Health, Imperial College London, UK
juliette.unwin@bristol.ac.uk
[5] School of Mathematics, University of Bristol, Bristol, UK
[6] Machine Learning and Global Health Network, UK
https://mlgh.net/

Abstract. Model-based disease mapping remains a fundamental policy-informing tool in the fields of public health and disease surveillance. Hierarchical Bayesian models have emerged as the state-of-the-art approach for disease mapping since they are able to both capture structure in the data and robustly characterise uncertainty. When working with areal data, e.g. aggregates at the administrative unit level such as district or province, current models rely on the adjacency structure of areal units to account for spatial correlations and perform shrinkage. The goal of disease surveillance systems is to track disease outcomes over time. This task is especially challenging in crisis situations which often lead to redrawn administrative boundaries, meaning that data collected before and after the crisis are no longer directly comparable. Moreover, the adjacency-based approach ignores the continuous nature of spatial processes and cannot solve the change-of-support problem, i.e. when estimates are required to be produced at different administrative levels or levels of aggregation. We present a novel, practical, and easy to implement solution to solve these problems relying on a methodology combining deep generative modelling and fully Bayesian inference: we build on the recently proposed PriorVAE method able to encode spatial priors over small areas with variational autoencoders by encoding aggregates over administrative units. We map malaria prevalence in Kenya, a country in which administrative boundaries changed in 2010.

Keywords: MCMC · VAE · Disease mapping

Bag of Policies for Distributional Deep Exploration

Asen Nachkov[1], Luchen Li[1] ⬤, Giulia Luise[1], Filippo Valdettaro[1] ⬤,
and A. Aldo Faisal[1,2] ⬤

[1] Brain & Behaviour Lab, Department of Computing, Imperial College London, London, SW7
2AZ UK
a.t.nachkov@gmail.com, {filippo.valdettaro20,
a.faisal}@imperial.ac.uk
[2] Chair in Digital Health & Data Science, University of Bayreuth, 95447 Bayreuth, Germany

Abstract. Efficient exploration in complex environments remains a
major challenge for reinforcement learning (RL). Compared to previous Thompson sampling-inspired mechanisms that enable temporally
extended exploration, i.e., deep exploration, we focus on deep exploration in distributional RL. We develop a general purpose approach, Bag
of Policies (BoP), that can be built on top of any return distribution estimator by maintaining a population of its copies. BoP consists of an ensemble
of multiple heads that are updated independently. During training, each
episode is controlled by only one of the heads and the collected state-
action pairs are used to update all heads off-policy, leading to distinct
learning signals for each head which diversify learning and behaviour.
To test whether optimistic ensemble method can improve on distributional RL as it does on scalar RL, we implement the BoP approach with
a population of distributional actor-critics using Bayesian Distributional
Policy Gradients (BDPG). The population thus approximates a posterior
distribution of return distributions along with a posterior distribution of
policies. Our setup allows to analyze global posterior uncertainty along
with local curiosity bonus simultaneously for exploration. As BDPG is
already an optimistic method, this pairing helps to investigate the extent to
which accumulating curiosity bonuses is beneficial. Overall BoP results
in greater robustness and speed during learning as demonstrated by our
experimental results on ALE Atari games.

Keywords: Distributional RL · Exploration · Intrinsic motivation

Defensive Perception: Estimation and Monitoring of Neural Network Performance under Deployment

Hendrik Vogt[1], Stefan Buehler[1], and Mark Schutera[1,2]

[1] ZF Friedrichshafen AG, Friedrichshafen, Germany
{hendrik.vogt,stefan.buehler}@zf.com, mark.schutera@kit.edu
[2] Karlsruhe Institute of Technology, Karlsruhe, Germany

Abstract. In this paper, we propose a method for addressing the issue of unnoticed catastrophic deployment and domain shift in neural networks for semantic segmentation in autonomous driving. Our approach is based on the idea that deep learning-based perception for autonomous driving is uncertain and best represented as a probability distribution. As autonomous vehicles' safety is paramount, it is crucial for perception systems to recognize when the vehicle is leaving its operational design domain, anticipate hazardous uncertainty, and reduce the performance of the perception system. To address this, we propose to encapsulate the neural network under deployment within an uncertainty estimation envelope that is based on the epistemic uncertainty estimation through the Monte Carlo Dropout approach. This approach does not require modification of the deployed neural network and guarantees expected model performance. Our *defensive perception envelope* has the capability to estimate a neural network's performance, enabling monitoring and notification of entering domains of reduced neural network performance under deployment. Furthermore, our envelope is extended by novel methods to improve the application in deployment settings, including reducing compute expenses and confining estimation noise. Finally, we demonstrate the applicability of our method for multiple different potential deployment shifts relevant to autonomous driving, such as transitions into the night, rainy, or snowy domain. Overall, our approach shows great potential for application in deployment settings and enables operational design domain recognition via uncertainty, which allows for defensive perception, safe state triggers, warning notifications, and feedback for testing or development and adaptation of the perception stack.

Keywords: Autonomous Driving · Safety Envelope · Computer Vision · Monte Carlo Dropout · Epistemic Uncertainty

Towards Understanding the Interplay of Generative Artificial Intelligence and the Internet

Gonzalo Martínez[1] , Lauren Watson[2] , Pedro Reviriego[3] ,
José Alberto Hernández[1] , Marc Juarez[2] , and Rik Sarkar[2]

[1] Universidad Carlos III de Madrid, Madrid, Spain
gonzmart@pa.uc3m.es, jahgutie@it.uc3m.es
[2] School of Informatics, University of Edinburgh, UK
{lauren.watson,marc.juarez,rik.sarkar}@ed.ac.uk
[3] Universidad Politécnica de Madrid, Madrid, Spain
pedro.reviriego@upm.es

Abstract. The rapid adoption of generative Artificial Intelligence (AI) tools that can generate realistic images or text, such as DALL-E, Mid-Journey, or ChatGPT, have put the societal impacts of these technologies at the center of public debate. These tools are possible due to the massive amount of data (text and images) that is publicly available through the Internet. At the same time, these generative AI tools become content creators that are already contributing to the data that is available to train future models. Therefore, future versions of generative AI tools will be trained with a mix of human-created and AI-generated content, causing a potential feedback loop between generative AI and public data repositories. This interaction raises many questions: how will future versions of generative AI tools behave when trained on a mixture of real and AI-generated data? Will they evolve and improve with the new data sets or on the contrary will they degrade? Will evolution introduce biases or reduce diversity in subsequent generations of generative AI tools? What are the societal implications of the possible degradation of these models? Can we mitigate the effects of this feedback loop? In this work, we explore the effect of this interaction and report some initial results using simple diffusion models trained with various image datasets. Our results show that the quality and diversity of the generated images can degrade over time suggesting that incorporating AI-created data can have undesired effects on future versions of generative models.

Keywords: Generative AI · Internet · Degeneration

Optimizing Brain Tumor Classification: A Comprehensive Study on Transfer Learning and Imbalance Handling in Deep Learning Models

Raza Imam[1,3] and Mohammed Talha Alam[2,3]

[1] Aligarh Muslim University, Aligarh, India
raza.imam@mbzuai.ac.ae
[2] Jamia Hamdard University, New Delhi, India
mohammed.alam@mbzuai.ac.ae
[3] Mohamed Bin Zayed University of Artificial Intelligence, Abu Dhabi, UAE

Abstract. Deep learning has emerged as a prominent field in recent literature, showcasing the introduction of models that utilize transfer learning to achieve remarkable accuracies in the classification of brain tumor MRI images. However, the majority of these proposals primarily focus on balanced datasets, neglecting the inherent data imbalance present in real-world scenarios. Consequently, there is a pressing need for approaches that not only address the data imbalance but also prioritize precise classification of brain cancer. In this work, we present a novel deep learning-based approach, called Transfer Learning-CNN, for brain tumor classification using MRI data. The proposed model leverages the predictive capabilities of existing publicly available models by utilizing their pre-trained weights and transferring those weights to the CNN. By leveraging a publicly available Brain MRI dataset, the experiment evaluated various transfer learning models for classifying different tumor types, including meningioma, glioma, and pituitary tumors. We investigate the impact of different loss functions, including focal loss, and oversampling methods, such as SMOTE and ADASYN, in addressing the data imbalance issue. Notably, the proposed strategy, which combines VGG-16 and CNN, achieved an impressive accuracy rate of 96%, surpassing alternative approaches significantly. Our code is available at Github.

Towards Offline Reinforcement Learning with Pessimistic Value Priors

Filippo Valdettaro[1] and A. Aldo Faisal[2]

[1] Brain & Behaviour Lab, Department of Computing, Imperial College London, London, SW7 2AZ, UK
filippo.valdettaro20@imperial.ac.uk
[2] Chair in Digital Health & Data Science, University of Bayreuth, 95447, Bayreuth, Germany
a.faisal@imperial.ac.uk

Abstract. Offline reinforcement learning (RL) seeks to train agents in sequential decision-making tasks using only previously collected data and without directly interacting with the environment. As the agent tries to improve on the policy present in the dataset, it can introduce distributional shift between the training data and the suggested agent's policy which can lead to poor performance. To avoid the agent assigning high values to out-of-distribution actions, successful offline RL requires some form of conservatism to be introduced. Here we present a model-free inference framework that encodes this conservatism in the prior belief of the value function: by carrying out policy evaluation with a pessimistic prior, we ensure that only the actions that are directly supported by the offline dataset will be modelled as having a high value. In contrast to other methods, we do not need to introduce heuristic policy constraints, value regularisation or uncertainty penalties to achieve successful offline RL policies in a toy environment. An additional consequence of our work is a principled quantification of Bayesian uncertainty in off-policy returns in model-free RL. While we are able to present an implementation of this framework to verify its behaviour in the exact inference setting with Gaussian processes on a toy problem, the scalability issues that it suffers as the central avenue for further work. We address in more detail these limitations and consider future directions to improve the scalability of this framework beyond the vanilla Gaussian process implementation, proposing a path towards improving offline RL algorithms in a principled way.

Semantic Attribution For Explainable Uncertainty Quantification

Hanjing Wang[1], Shiqiang Wang[2], and Qiang Ji[1]

[1] Rensselaer Polytechnic Institute, Troy, NY, USA
{wangh36,jiq}@rpi.edu
[2] IBM Thomas J. Watson Research Center, Yorktown Heights, NY, USA
wangshiq@us.ibm.com

Abstract. Bayesian deep learning, with an emphasis on uncertainty quantification, is receiving growing interest in building reliable models. Nonetheless, interpreting and explaining the origins and reasons for uncertainty presents a significant challenge. In this paper, we present semantic uncertainty attribution as a tool for pinpointing the primary factors contributing to uncertainty. This approach allows us to explain why a particular image carries high uncertainty, thereby making our models more interpretable. Specifically, we utilize the variational autoencoder to disentangle different semantic factors within the latent space and link the uncertainty to corresponding semantic factors for an explanation. The proposed techniques can also enhance explainable out-of-distribution (OOD) detection. We can not only identify OOD samples via their uncertainty, but also provide reasoning rooted in a semantic concept.

Keywords: Bayesian Deep Learning · Uncertainty Attribution

Contents

A Novel Bayes' Theorem for Upper Probabilities

Michele Caprio[1]([✉]), Yusuf Sale[2,3], Eyke Hüllermeier[2,3], and Insup Lee[1]

[1] University of Pennsylvania, Philadelphia, PA 19104, USA
`{caprio,lee}@seas.upenn.edu`
[2] University of Munich (LMU), 80539 Munich, Germany
`{yusuf.sale,eyke}@lmu.de`
[3] Munich Center for Machine Learning, 80539 Munich, Germany

Abstract. In their seminal 1990 paper, Wasserman and Kadane establish an upper bound for the Bayes' posterior probability of a measurable set A, when the prior lies in a class of probability measures $\mathcal{P}$ and the likelihood is precise. They also give a sufficient condition for such upper bound to hold with equality. In this paper, we introduce a generalization of their result by additionally addressing uncertainty related to the likelihood. We give an upper bound for the posterior probability when both the prior and the likelihood belong to a set of probabilities. Furthermore, we give a sufficient condition for this upper bound to become an equality. This result is interesting on its own, and has the potential of being applied to various fields of engineering (e.g. model predictive control), machine learning, and artificial intelligence.

Keywords: Probabilistic Machine Learning · Credal Sets · Robust Machine Learning · Imprecise Probabilities · Bayesian inference

1 Introduction

Bayes' rule (BR) is arguably the best-known mechanism to update subjective beliefs. It prescribes the agent to elicit a prior distribution that encapsulates their initial opinion, and to come up with a likelihood that describes the data generating process. Combining prior and likelihood via BR produces the posterior distribution, which captures the agent's revised opinion in light of the collected data.

But what happens if the agent is not able to specify a single prior distribution? This may occur if they face *ambiguity* [9,14]. In [29, Section 1.1.4] and [4], the authors point out that missing information and bounded rationality may prevent the agent from assessing probabilities precisely in practice, even if doing so is possible in principle. This may be due to the lack of information on how likely events of interest are, lack of computational time or ability, or because it is extremely difficult to analyze a complex body of evidence. Similarly, the agent may face difficulties in gauging the data generating process, so specifying a single likelihood may become a challenging task.

F. Cuzzolin and M. Sultana (Eds.): Epi UAI 2023, LNAI 14523, pp. 1–12, 2024.
https://doi.org/10.1007/978-3-031-57963-9_1

The notion of ambiguity is strictly related with that of epistemic uncertainty in machine learning (ML) and artificial intelligence (AI). Let us illustrate this clearly by borrowing concepts from [3, Section 3.2]. Epistemic uncertainty (EU) corresponds to reducible uncertainty caused by a lack of knowledge about the best model. Notice how, in the precise case – that is, when the agent specifies a single distribution – EU is absent. In many applications, a single probability measure is only able to capture the idea of irreducible uncertainty, since it represents a case in which the agent knows exactly the true data generating process, and the prior probability that perfectly encapsulates their initial beliefs. This is a well-studied property of sets of probabilities [18, Page 458]. Due to the increasing relevance of reliable and trustworthy ML and AI applications, effective uncertainty representation and quantification have become vital research areas [8,19,20,25,26,31]. Thus, theoretic underpinnings of imprecise probability theories emerge as a valuable methodology for improving the representation and quantification of uncertainties. Adopting concepts like (convex) sets of probabilities and upper and lower probabilities foster a more sophisticated and fine-tuned articulation of uncertainty.

We remark that EU should not be confused with the concept of *epistemic probability* [11,12,29]. In the subjective probability literature, epistemic probability can be captured by a single distribution. Its best definition can be found in [29, Sections 1.3.2 and 2.11.2]. There, the author specifies how epistemic probabilities model logical or psychological degrees of partial belief of the agent. We remark, though, how de Finetti and Walley work with finitely additive probabilities, while in this paper we use countably additive probabilities.

The field of imprecise probabilities [1,29], and in particular the classic paper by [30], and successive works like [7,10,13,21], study the problem of an agent updating their beliefs using BR in the presence of ambiguity. Our paper belongs to this body of work. Our main result, Theorem 1, generalizes the theorem in [30, Section 2] to the case where the agent faces ambiguity on both what prior and what likelihood to choose to model the phenomenon of interest. We find the upper posterior, that is, the "upper bound" to the set of posteriors, using only the upper prior and the upper likelihood. Thanks to the conjugacy property of upper probabilities, introduced in the next section, we derive the lower posterior, that is the "lower bound" to the set of posteriors. We also give a necessary condition for the bound to hold with equality. In addition, we hint at possible applications, in particular in the field of model predictive control, a method of process control that is used to control a process while satisfying a set of constraints [23].

The paper is divided as follows. Section 2.1 introduces the concepts that are needed to understand our result. In Sect. 2.2 we present the main theorem, and conclude our work Sect. 3. We prove our results in Sect. 4.

2 Bayes' Theorem for Upper Probabilities

2.1 Preliminaries

In this section, we introduce the background notions from the IP literature [1, 27, 29] that are needed to understand our main results.

Call $\Delta(\Omega, \mathcal{F})$ the space of (countably additive) probability measures on a generic measurable space $(\Omega, \mathcal{F})$. Pick a generic set $\mathcal{P} \subset \Delta(\Omega, \mathcal{F})$. We denote by $\overline{P}$ the *upper probability* associated with $\mathcal{P}$, that is, $\overline{P}(A) = \sup_{P \in \mathcal{P}} P(A)$, for all $A \in \mathcal{F}$. Its conjugate is called *lower probability*, $\underline{P}(A) = 1 - \overline{P}(A^c) = \inf_{P \in \mathcal{P}} P(A)$, for all $A \in \mathcal{F}$. Because of the conjugacy property, in the remainder of this document we focus on upper probabilities only.

We say that upper probability $\overline{P}$ is *concave* or *2-alternating* if $\overline{P}(A \cup B) \leq \overline{P}(A) + \overline{P}(B) - \overline{P}(A \cap B)$, for all $A, B \in \mathcal{F}$. Upper probability $\overline{P}$ is *compatible* [15] with the set

$$\text{core}(\overline{P}) := \{P \in \Delta(\Omega, \mathcal{F}) : P(A) \leq \overline{P}(A), \forall A \in \mathcal{F}\}$$
$$= \{P \in \Delta(\Omega, \mathcal{F}) : \overline{P}(A) \geq P(A) \geq \underline{P}(A),$$
$$\forall A \in \mathcal{F}\} \tag{1}$$

where (1) is a characterization [6, Page 3389]. The core is the set of all (countably additive) probability measures on Ω that are set-wise dominated by $\overline{P}$. It is convex: it is immediate to see that if P and Q are dominated by $\overline{P}$, then γP and $(1-\gamma)Q$ are dominated by $\gamma \overline{P}$ and $(1-\gamma)\overline{P}$, respectively, for all $\gamma \in [0, 1]$. In turn, $\gamma P + (1 - \gamma)Q$ is dominated by $\overline{P}$, thus giving the desired convex property. In addition, throughout the present work, we assume that $\text{core}(\overline{P})$ is nonempty and weak*-closed.[1] Then, as a result of [29, Section 3.6.1], it is also weak*-compact.

Remark 1. In [29, Section 3.6.1], the author shows that the finitely additive core is weak*-compact. The latter is defined as the set of all *finitely additive* probabilities that are set-wise dominated by $\overline{P}$. It is a superset of the countably additive core in (1). To see this, notice that, in general, there might well be a probability measure that is set-wise dominated by $\overline{P}$, but that is merely finitely additive. In fact, there might even be no countably additive probabilities that are set-wise dominated by $\overline{P}$. For this reason, we have to assume that the countably additive core in (1) is nonempty. If we further require that the countably additive core in (1) is weak*-closed, then, this implies that it is a weak*-closed subset of a weak*-compact space. By [24, Theorem 2.35], closed subsets of compact sets are compact. In turn, we have that if the countably additive core is weak*-closed, it is also weak*-compact.

We now present a class of probabilities that (i) is well-studied and used in robust statistics [17], and (ii) is the core of a concave upper probability. Other classes with similar properties are presented in [30, Examples 3–7].

---

[1] Recall that in the weak* topology, a net $(P_\alpha)_{\alpha \in I}$ converges to P if and only if $P_\alpha(A) \to P(A)$, for all $A \in \mathcal{F}$. See also results presented in [29, Appendix D3].

Example 1 (ε-contaminated class). Consider the space $\Delta(\Omega, \mathcal{F})$ of probability measures on a generic measurable space $(\Omega, \mathcal{F})$, and assume Ω is compact. Pick any $P \in \Delta(\Omega, \mathcal{F})$ and any $\varepsilon \in [0,1]$. Define

$$\mathcal{Q}^{\mathrm{co}} := \{Q \in \Delta(\Omega, \mathcal{F}) : Q(A) = (1-\varepsilon)P(A) + \varepsilon R(A),$$
$$\forall A \in \mathcal{F},\ R \in \Delta(\Omega, \mathcal{F})\}. \tag{2}$$

Superscript "co" stands for convex and core. $\mathcal{Q}^{\mathrm{co}}$ is the ε-contaminated class induced by P; it was studied in [30, Example 3] and references therein. We have that $\overline{Q}(A) = (1-\varepsilon)P(A) + \varepsilon$, for all $A \in \mathcal{F}\setminus\{\emptyset\}$ and $\underline{Q}(A) = (1-\varepsilon)P(A)$, for all $A \in \mathcal{F}\setminus\{\Omega\}$. In addition, $\mathcal{Q}^{\mathrm{co}} = \mathrm{core}(\overline{Q})$, and $\overline{Q}$ is concave.

The ε-contaminated class is also instrumental for a future application of Theorem 1 to model predictive control. We will discuss this at length at the end of Sect. 2.2. There, we also explain why it is important to account for the ambiguity in the likelihood model in real-world safety-critical scenarios.

2.2   A Novel Bayes' Theorem for Upper Probabilities

Let $(\Theta, \mathcal{F})$ be the measurable parameter space of interest and $\Delta(\Theta, \mathcal{F})$ the space of (countably additive) probability measures on $(\Theta, \mathcal{F})$. Let $\mathcal{Y}$ be the set of all *bounded, non-negative,* $\mathcal{F}$-measurable functionals on Θ. Call $\mathscr{D}$ the sample space endowed with sigma-algebra $\mathcal{A}$. That is, for any random variable Y of interest and all $\theta \in \Theta$, $Y(\theta) = y \in \mathscr{D}$. Let the agent elicit a set of probabilities $\mathcal{L}_\theta := \{P_\theta \in \Delta(\mathscr{D}, \mathcal{A}) : \theta \in \Theta\}$ on $\mathscr{D}$, parameterized by $\theta \in \Theta$. This captures the ambiguity faced by the agent in determining the true data generating process [9,14]. We write $P_\theta \equiv P(\cdot \mid \theta)$ for notational convenience. Assume that each $P_\theta \in \mathcal{L}_\theta$ has density $L(\theta) = p(y \mid \theta)$ with respect to some sigma-finite dominating measure ν on $(\mathscr{D}, \mathcal{A})$; this represents the likelihood function for θ having observed data $y \in \mathscr{D}$.

Assumption 1. Every density L corresponding to an element P_θ of $\mathcal{L}_\theta$ belongs to $\mathcal{Y}$; that is, every density is bounded and non-negative.

Assumption 1 is needed mainly for mathematical purposes; as we shall see later in this section, it can be relaxed. Let the agent specify a set $\mathcal{P}$ of probabilities on $(\Theta, \mathcal{F})$. It represents their (incomplete) prior knowledge on the elements of $\mathcal{F}$; its elements may be informed by the collected data, thus giving the analysis an (imprecise) empirical Bayes flavor [5]. Then, compute $\overline{P}(A) = \sup_{P \in \mathcal{P}} P(A)$, for all $A \in \mathcal{F}$, and consider $\mathcal{P}^{\mathrm{co}} := \mathrm{core}(\overline{P})$, assumed nonempty and weak*-closed. It represents the agent's initial beliefs. We assume that every $P \in \mathcal{P}^{\mathrm{co}}$ has density p with respect to some sigma-finite dominating measure μ on $(\Theta, \mathcal{F})$, that is, $p = \mathrm{d}P/\mathrm{d}\mu$. We require the agent's beliefs to be represented by the core for two main reasons. The first, mathematical, one is to ensure that the upper probability is compatible with the belief set. The second, philosophical, one is the following. In Bayesian statistics, the agent selects a specific prior to encapsulate their initial beliefs. [2] points out how such choice is oftentimes arbitrary, and posits the *dogma of ideal precision* (DIP). It states that in any problem there is an *ideal probability model* P_T which is precise, but which may not be precisely known. To overcome this shortcoming, the agent should specify a finite collection $\{P_s\}_{s \in S}$ of "plausible" prior distributions, and compute the posterior for each P_s. Notice how this corresponds to selecting a finite number of elements from the core of $\overline{P}_S$, where $\overline{P}_S(A) = \sup_{s \in S} P_s(A)$, for all $A \in \mathcal{F}$. A criticism to the DIP was brought forward by Walley. In [29, Section 2.10.4.(c)], he claims how given an upper probability $\overline{P}$, there is no cogent reason for which the agent should choose a specific P_T that is dominated by $\overline{P}$, or – for that matter – a collection $\{P_s\}_{s \in S}$ of "plausible" probabilities. Because the core considers all (countably additive) probability measures that are dominated by $\overline{P}$, it is the perfect instrument to address Walley's criticism [4].

Let the agent compute $\overline{P}_\theta$, the upper probability associated with $\mathcal{L}_\theta$, and consider $\mathcal{L}_\theta^{co} := \text{core}(\overline{P}_\theta)$, assumed nonempty and weak*-closed. It represents the set of plausible likelihoods. As [16] point out, accounting for ambiguity around the true data generating process is crucial, as Bayesian inference may suffer from inconsistency issues if carried out using a misspecified likelihood.

Let

$$\mathscr{L} := \left\{ L = \frac{\mathrm{d}P_\theta}{\mathrm{d}\nu}, \, P_\theta \in \mathcal{L}_\theta^{co} \right\} \subset \mathcal{Y} \tag{3}$$

be the set of pdf/pmf associated with the elements of $\mathcal{L}_\theta^{co}$. Let also $\overline{L}(\theta) := \sup_{L \in \mathscr{L}} L(\theta)$ and $\underline{L}(\theta) := \inf_{L \in \mathscr{L}} L(\theta)$, for all $\theta \in \Theta$. Call

$$\mathcal{P}_y^{co} := \left\{ P_y \in \Delta(\Theta, \mathcal{F}) : \right.$$

$$\frac{\mathrm{d}P_y}{\mathrm{d}\mu} = p(\theta \mid y) = \frac{L(\theta)p(\theta)}{\int_\Theta L(\theta)p(\theta)\mathrm{d}\theta},$$

$$\left. p = \frac{\mathrm{d}P}{\mathrm{d}\mu}, \, P \in \mathcal{P}^{co}, \, L = \frac{\mathrm{d}P_\theta}{\mathrm{d}\nu}, \, P_\theta \in \mathcal{L}_\theta^{co} \right\}$$

the class of posterior probabilities when the prior is in $\mathcal{P}^{co}$ and the likelihood is in $\mathcal{L}_\theta^{co}$, and let $\overline{P}_y(A) = \sup_{P_y \in \mathcal{P}_y^{co}} P_y(A)$, for all $A \in \mathcal{F}$. Then, the following is a generalization of Bayes' theorem in [30, Section 2], and is an extension of [3, Theorem 7]. We prove it in Sect. 4.

Theorem 1 (Bayes' theorem for upper probabilities). *Suppose* $\mathcal{P}^{co}, \mathcal{L}_\theta^{co}$ *are nonempty and weak*-closed. Then for all* $A \in \mathcal{F}$,

$$\overline{P}_y(A) \leq \frac{\sup_{P \in \mathcal{P}^{co}} \int_\Theta \overline{L}(\theta)\mathbb{1}_A(\theta)P(\mathrm{d}\theta)}{\mathbf{c}} \tag{4}$$

$$\leq \frac{\int_0^\infty \overline{P}\left(\{\theta \in \Theta : \overline{L}(\theta)\mathbb{1}_A(\theta) > t\}\right)\mathrm{d}t}{\mathbf{c}'}, \tag{5}$$

provided that the ratios are well defined. Here $\mathbb{1}_A$ *denotes the indicator function for* $A \in \mathcal{F}$, $\mathbf{c} := \sup_{P \in \mathcal{P}^{co}} \int_\Theta \overline{L}(\theta)\mathbb{1}_A(\theta)P(\mathrm{d}\theta) + \inf_{P \in \mathcal{P}^{co}} \int_\Theta \underline{L}(\theta)\mathbb{1}_{A^c}(\theta)P(\mathrm{d}\theta)$, *and*

$$\mathbf{c}' := \underbrace{\int_0^\infty \overline{P}\left(\{\theta \in \Theta : \overline{L}(\theta)\mathbb{1}_A(\theta) > t\}\right) dt}_{\textit{upper Choquet integral of } \overline{L}\mathbb{1}_A}$$

$$+ \underbrace{\int_0^\infty \underline{P}\left(\{\theta \in \Theta : \underline{L}(\theta)\mathbb{1}_{A^c}(\theta) > t\}\right) dt}_{\textit{lower Choquet integral of } \underline{L}\mathbb{1}_{A^c}}.$$

In addition, if $\overline{P}$ is concave, then the inequalities in (4) and (5) are equalities, for all $A \in \mathcal{F}$.

This result is particularly appealing. Under Assumption 1, if the prior upper probability (PUP) is concave and the prior and likelihood sets $\mathcal{P}^{co}, \mathcal{L}_\theta^{co}$ are nonempty and weak*-closed, then the agent can perform a (generalized) Bayesian update of the PUP by carrying out only one operation. This is the case even when the agent faces ambiguity around the true data generating process so that a set of likelihoods is needed. The posterior lower probability is obtained immediately via the conjugacy property $\underline{P}_y(A) = 1 - \overline{P}_y(A^c)$.

Corollary 1. *Retain the assumptions in Theorem 1. If $\mathcal{L}_\theta^{co}$ is a singleton, we retrieve Bayes' theorem in [30, Section 2].*

Corollary 1 tell us that when there is no ambiguity around the likelihood, Theorem 1 recovers Wasserman and Kadane's classical Bayes' theorem. Given the straightforward nature of the proof, we omit it here. We also have the following lemma, that is proved in Sect. 4.

Lemma 1 (Preserved concavity). *Suppose $\mathcal{P}^{co}, \mathcal{L}_\theta^{co}$ are nonempty and weak*-closed. Then, if $\overline{P}$ is concave, we have that $\overline{P}_y$ is concave as well.*

This lemma is important because it tells us that the generalized Bayesian update of Theorem 1 preserves concavity, and so it can be applied to successive iterations. If at time t the PUP is concave, then the PUP at time $t + 1$ – that is, the posterior upper probability at time t – will be concave too. Necessary and sufficient conditions for a generic upper probability to be concave are given in [22, Section 5].

In the future, we plan to forego Assumption 1 and use the techniques developed in [27] to generalize our results to the case in which the elements of $\mathcal{L}$ are unbounded and not necessarily non-negative. We also intend to extend our results to the case in which the elements of $\mathcal{Y}$ are $\mathbb{R}^d$-valued, for some $d \in \mathbb{N}$. We suspect this is a less demanding endeavor since we do not use specific properties of $\mathbb{R}$ in our proofs.

As mentioned earlier, a natural application of our results is model predictive control (MPC). MPC is a method that is used to control a process while satisfying a set of constraints [23]. Typically, when the process is stable (or at least stable for the past k time steps, for some $k \geq 0$) and if the scholar decides to take the Bayesian approach, they proceed as follows. They specify a Normal likelihood (the distribution of the control inputs) centered at the objective function of the process, and a Normal prior on the parameter of such function. In this framework, if ambiguity enters the picture, then our results become relevant.

The importance of addressing prior ambiguity was discussed at length in Sect. 2.2. The reasons why accounting for likelihood ambiguity is important are as follows. First, as pointed out earlier, we may run into inconsistency issues if we perform Bayesian analysis using a misspecified likelihood [16]. Second, a (precise) Normal likelihood is a good choice only if stability of the process is ensured. MPC procedures are used in the process industries in chemical plants, oil refineries, power system balancing models, and power electronics. These are all safety-critical applications where accounting for possible sudden unexpected instabilities is of paramount importance.

The scholar may specify a class of ϵ-contaminated truncated Normal priors and a class of η-contaminated truncated Normal likelihoods, and use Theorem 1 to compute the upper posterior. Notice that the Normals need to be truncated in light of Assumption 1. This requirement is not too stringent, and – as pointed out earlier in this section – our future work will allow us do without it.

3 Conclusion

In this paper, we present a new Bayes' theorem for upper probabilities that extends the one in [30, Section 2], and [3, Theorem 7]. In the future, we plan to generalize Theorem 1 by letting go of Assumption 1, and to apply it to an MPC problem and to other fields of engineering, and ML and AI. For example, we intend to use it to overcome the computational bottleneck of step 2 of the algorithm that computes the posterior set in an imprecise Bayesian neural network procedure [3]. There, an element-wise application of Bayes' rule for all the extreme elements of the prior and likelihood sets is performed. As we can see, this is a combinatorial task that can potentially be greatly simplified in light of Theorem 1, conveying a computationally cheaper algorithm.

4 Proofs

Proof (Proof of Theorem 1). Assume that $\mathcal{P}^{co}, \mathcal{L}_\theta^{co}$ are nonempty and weak⋆-closed. Pick any $A \in \mathcal{F}$. Recall that we can rewrite the usual Bayes' updating rule as

$$P_y(A) = \frac{\int_\Theta L(\theta)\mathbb{1}_A(\theta)P(\mathrm{d}\theta)}{\int_\Theta L(\theta)\mathbb{1}_A(\theta)P(\mathrm{d}\theta) + \int_\Theta L(\theta)\mathbb{1}_{A^c}(\theta)P(\mathrm{d}\theta)}$$

$$= \frac{1}{1 + \frac{\int_\Theta L(\theta)\mathbb{1}_{A^c}(\theta)P(\mathrm{d}\theta)}{\int_\Theta L(\theta)\mathbb{1}_A(\theta)P(\mathrm{d}\theta)}},$$

which is maximized when

$$\frac{\int_\Theta L(\theta)\mathbb{1}_{A^c}(\theta)P(\mathrm{d}\theta)}{\int_\Theta L(\theta)\mathbb{1}_A(\theta)P(\mathrm{d}\theta)}$$

is minimized. But

$$\frac{\int_\Theta L(\theta)\mathbb{1}_{A^c}(\theta)P(\mathrm{d}\theta)}{\int_\Theta L(\theta)\mathbb{1}_A(\theta)P(\mathrm{d}\theta)} \geq \frac{\inf_{P\in\mathcal{P}^{\mathrm{co}}}\int_\Theta \underline{L}(\theta)\mathbb{1}_{A^c}(\theta)P(\mathrm{d}\theta)}{\sup_{P\in\mathcal{P}^{\mathrm{co}}}\int_\Theta \overline{L}(\theta)\mathbb{1}_A(\theta)P(\mathrm{d}\theta)},$$

which proves the inequality in (4). The inequality in (5) is true because

$$\inf_{P\in\mathcal{P}^{\mathrm{co}}}\int_\Theta \underline{L}(\theta)\mathbb{1}_{A^c}(\theta)P(\mathrm{d}\theta)$$
$$\geq \int_0^\infty \underline{P}(\{\theta\in\Theta:\underline{L}(\theta)\mathbb{1}_{A^c}(\theta)>t\})\,\mathrm{d}t$$

and

$$\sup_{P\in\mathcal{P}^{\mathrm{co}}}\int_\Theta \overline{L}(\theta)\mathbb{1}_A(\theta)P(\mathrm{d}\theta)$$
$$\leq \int_0^\infty \overline{P}(\{\theta\in\Theta:\overline{L}(\theta)\mathbb{1}_A(\theta)>t\})\,\mathrm{d}t.$$

Assume now that $\overline{P}$ is concave. By [30, Lemma 1], we have that there exists $\check{P}\in\mathcal{P}^{\mathrm{co}}$ such that

$$\sup_{P\in\mathcal{P}^{\mathrm{co}}}\int_\Theta L(\theta)\mathbb{1}_A(\theta)P(\mathrm{d}\theta) = \int_\Theta L(\theta)\mathbb{1}_A(\theta)\check{P}(\mathrm{d}\theta), \qquad (6)$$

for all $L\in\mathcal{L}$. In addition, by [30, Lemma 4], we have that for all $Y\in\mathcal{Y}$ and all $\epsilon>0$, there exists a non-negative, upper semi-continuous function $h\leq Y$ such that

$$\left[\sup_{P\in\mathcal{P}^{\mathrm{co}}}\int_\Theta Y(\theta)P(\mathrm{d}\theta)\right] - \epsilon < \sup_{P\in\mathcal{P}^{\mathrm{co}}}\int_\Theta h(\theta)P(\mathrm{d}\theta)$$
$$\leq \sup_{P\in\mathcal{P}^{\mathrm{co}}}\int_\Theta Y(\theta)P(\mathrm{d}\theta). \qquad (7)$$

Let now $Y = \overline{L}\mathbb{1}_A$. Notice that since $\mathcal{L}_\theta^{\mathrm{co}}$ is weak*-compact (as a result of [29, Section 3.6.1]), by (3) so is $\mathcal{L}$. This implies that $\underline{L},\overline{L}\in\mathcal{L}$, since a compact set always contains its boundary, so $\underline{L},\overline{L}\in\mathcal{Y}$ as well, and in turn $\underline{L}\mathbb{1}_{A^c},\overline{L}\mathbb{1}_A\in\mathcal{Y}$. Fix then any $L\in\mathcal{L}$ and put $h = L\mathbb{1}_A$. It is immediate to see that h is non-negative and upper semi-continuous. Then, by (7), we have that for all $\epsilon>0$

$$\left[\sup_{P\in\mathcal{P}^{\mathrm{co}}}\int_\Theta \overline{L}(\theta)\mathbb{1}_A(\theta)P(\mathrm{d}\theta)\right] - \epsilon <$$
$$\sup_{P\in\mathcal{P}^{\mathrm{co}}}\int_\Theta L(\theta)\mathbb{1}_A(\theta)P(\mathrm{d}\theta) \leq \sup_{P\in\mathcal{P}^{\mathrm{co}}}\int_\Theta \overline{L}(\theta)\mathbb{1}_A(\theta)P(\mathrm{d}\theta). \qquad (8)$$

Combining (6) and (8), we obtain

$$
\left[\sup_{P \in \mathcal{P}^{co}} \int_{\Theta} \overline{L}(\theta) \mathbb{1}_A(\theta) P(d\theta) \right] - \epsilon
$$
$$
< \int_{\Theta} L(\theta) \mathbb{1}_A(\theta) \check{P}(d\theta) \leq \sup_{P \in \mathcal{P}^{co}} \int_{\Theta} \overline{L}(\theta) \mathbb{1}_A(\theta) P(d\theta), \tag{9}
$$

for all $L \in \mathcal{L}$.

Pick now any $\epsilon > 0$ and put

$$
k := \sup_{P \in \mathcal{P}^{co}} \int_{\Theta} \overline{L}(\theta) \mathbb{1}_A(\theta) P(d\theta)
$$
$$
+ \inf_{P \in \mathcal{P}^{co}} \int_{\Theta} \underline{L}(\theta) \mathbb{1}_{A^c}(\theta) P(d\theta) > 0.
$$

Choose any $L \in \mathcal{L}$ and $\delta \in (0, \epsilon k)$. By (9) we have that

$$
\left[\sup_{P \in \mathcal{P}^{co}} \int_{\Theta} \overline{L}(\theta) \mathbb{1}_A(\theta) P(d\theta) \right] - \delta < \int_{\Theta} L(\theta) \mathbb{1}_A(\theta) \check{P}(d\theta) \tag{10}
$$

and that

$$
\left[\inf_{P \in \mathcal{P}^{co}} \int_{\Theta} \underline{L}(\theta) \mathbb{1}_{A^c}(\theta) P(d\theta) \right] + \delta > \int_{\Theta} L(\theta) \mathbb{1}_{A^c}(\theta) \check{P}(d\theta). \tag{11}
$$

The inequality in (10) comes from the fact that the first inequality in (9) holds for all $\epsilon > 0$, and – given how k is defined – we have that $\delta > 0$. The inequality in (11) is obtained by re-deriving (6), (7), (8), and (9) for the infimum of set $\mathcal{P}^{co}$ rather than the supremum. In that case, we simply substitute sup with inf, $\overline{L}$ with $\underline{L}$, $\mathbb{1}_A$ with $\mathbb{1}_{A^c}$, "$-\epsilon$" with "$+\epsilon$", and we reverse the inequalities.

Recall that

$$
\mathbf{c} := \sup_{P \in \mathcal{P}^{co}} \int_{\Theta} \overline{L}(\theta) \mathbb{1}_A(\theta) P(d\theta) + \inf_{P \in \mathcal{P}^{co}} \int_{\Theta} \underline{L}(\theta) \mathbb{1}_{A^c}(\theta) P(d\theta),
$$

and define

$$
\mathbf{d} := \int_{\Theta} L(\theta) \mathbb{1}_A(\theta) \check{P}(d\theta) + \int_{\Theta} L(\theta) \mathbb{1}_{A^c}(\theta) \check{P}(d\theta).
$$

Then we have,

$$
\check{P}_y(A) = \frac{\int_{\Theta} L(\theta) \mathbb{1}_A(\theta) \check{P}(d\theta)}{\mathbf{d}}
$$
$$
\geq \frac{\left[\sup_{P \in \mathcal{P}^{co}} \int_{\Theta} \overline{L}(\theta) \mathbb{1}_A(\theta) P(d\theta) \right] - \delta}{\mathbf{c} + \delta - \delta}
$$
$$
= \frac{\sup_{P \in \mathcal{P}^{co}} \int_{\Theta} \overline{L}(\theta) \mathbb{1}_A(\theta) P(d\theta)}{\mathbf{c}} - \frac{\delta}{k}
$$
$$
> \frac{\sup_{P \in \mathcal{P}^{co}} \int_{\Theta} \overline{L}(\theta) \mathbb{1}_A(\theta) P(d\theta)}{\mathbf{c}} - \epsilon.
$$

10   M. Caprio et al.

Since this holds for all $\epsilon > 0$, we have that

$$\sup_{P_y \in \mathcal{P}_y^{co}} P_y(A) = \frac{\sup_{P \in \mathcal{P}^{co}} \int_\Theta \overline{L}(\theta) \mathbb{1}_A(\theta) P(\mathrm{d}\theta)}{\mathbf{c}},$$

concluding the proof of inequality (4) being an equality when $\overline{P}$ is concave. Inequality (5) being an equality when $\overline{P}$ is concave comes immediately from [30, Lemma 4], and the fact that $\overline{L}\mathbb{1}_A, \underline{L}\mathbb{1}_{A^c} \in \mathcal{Y}$, as pointed out above.

Proof (Proof of Lemma 1). In their works [28,30], the authors show that concave upper probabilities are closed with respect to the generalized Bayes' rule. In particular, this means that, if we let $\mathbf{b} := \sup_{P \in \mathcal{P}^{co}} \int_\Theta L(\theta) \mathbb{1}_A(\theta) P(\mathrm{d}\theta) + \inf_{P \in \mathcal{P}^{co}} \int_\Theta L(\theta) \mathbb{1}_{A^c}(\theta) P(\mathrm{d}\theta)$, for any fixed $A \in \mathcal{F}$, if $\overline{P}$ is concave, then for all $L \in \mathcal{L}$

$$\overline{P}_y(A) = \frac{\sup_{P \in \mathcal{P}^{co}} \int_\Theta L(\theta) \mathbb{1}_A(\theta) P(\mathrm{d}\theta)}{\mathbf{b}} \tag{12}$$

is concave. But since $\mathcal{L}_\theta^{co}$ is weak*-compact (as a consequence of [29, Section 3.6.1]), by (3) so is $\mathcal{L}$. This implies that $\underline{L}, \overline{L} \in \mathcal{L}$, since a compact set always contains its boundary. Call then $L' = \overline{L}\mathbb{1}_A + \underline{L}\mathbb{1}_{A^c}$. It is immediate to see that $L' \in \mathcal{L}$. Then, by (12) we have that if we call

$$\mathbf{b}' := \sup_{P \in \mathcal{P}^{co}} \int_\Theta L'(\theta) \mathbb{1}_A(\theta) P(\mathrm{d}\theta) + \inf_{P \in \mathcal{P}^{co}} \int_\Theta L'(\theta) \mathbb{1}_{A^c}(\theta) P(\mathrm{d}\theta),$$

it follows that

$$\begin{aligned}
\overline{P}_y(A) &= \frac{\sup_{P \in \mathcal{P}^{co}} \int_\Theta L'(\theta) \mathbb{1}_A(\theta) P(\mathrm{d}\theta)}{\mathbf{b}'} \\
&= \frac{\sup_{P \in \mathcal{P}^{co}} \int_\Theta \overline{L}(\theta) \mathbb{1}_A(\theta) P(\mathrm{d}\theta)}{\mathbf{c}}
\end{aligned}$$

is concave, concluding the proof.

Acknowledgments. Michele Caprio would like to acknowledge partial funding by the Army Research Office (ARO MURI W911NF2010080). Yusuf Sale is supported by the DAAD programme Konrad Zuse Schools of Excellence in Artificial Intelligence, sponsored by the Federal Ministry of Education and Research.

Disclosure of Interests. The authors have no competing interests to declare that are relevant to the content of this article.

References

1. Augustin, T., Coolen, F.P.A., De Cooman, G., Troffaes, M.C.M. (eds.): Introduction to Imprecise Probabilities. Wiley Series in Probability and Statistics, Wiley, Hoboken (2014)

2. Berger, J.O.: The robust Bayesian viewpoint. In: Kadane, J.B. (ed.) Robustness of Bayesian Analyses. North-Holland, Amsterdam (1984)
3. Caprio, M., et al.: Imprecise Bayesian neural networks (2023). arXiv:2302.09656
4. Caprio, M., Gong, R.: Dynamic imprecise probability kinematics. In: Proceedings of Machine Learning Research, vol. 215, pp. 72–83 (2023)
5. Casella, G.: An introduction to empirical Bayes data analysis. Am. Stat. **39**(2), 83–87 (1985)
6. Cerreia-Vioglio, S., Maccheroni, F., Marinacci, M.: Ergodic theorems for lower probabilities. Proc. Am. Math. Soc. **144**, 3381–3396 (2015)
7. Cozman, F.G.: Credal networks. Artif. Intell. **120**, 199–233 (2000)
8. Depeweg, S., Hernandez-Lobato, J.M., Doshi-Velez, F., Udluft, S.: Decomposition of uncertainty in Bayesian deep learning for efficient and risk-sensitive learning. In: Dy, J., Krause, A. (eds.) Proceedings of the 35th International Conference on Machine Learning. Proceedings of Machine Learning Research, vol. 80, pp. 1184–1193. PMLR (2018)
9. Ellsberg, D.: Risk, ambiguity, and the Savage axioms. Q. J. Econ. **75**(4), 643–669 (1961)
10. Epstein, L.G., Wang, T.: Intertemporal asset pricing under Knightian uncertainty. Econometrica **62**(2), 283–322 (1994)
11. de Finetti, B.: Theory of Probability, vol. 1. Wiley, New York (1974)
12. de Finetti, B.: Theory of Probability, vol. 2. Wiley, New York (1975)
13. Giacomini, R., Kitagawa, T.: Robust Bayesian inference for set-identified models. Econometrica **89**(4), 1519–1556 (2021)
14. Gilboa, I., Marinacci, M.: Ambiguity and the Bayesian paradigm. In: Acemoglu, D., Arellano, M., Dekel, E. (eds.) Advances in Economics and Econometrics, Tenth World Congress, vol. 1. Cambridge University Press, Cambridge (2013)
15. Gong, R., Meng, X.L.: Judicious judgment meets unsettling updating: dilation, sure loss, and Simpson's paradox. Stat. Sci. **36**(2), 169–190 (2021)
16. Grünwald, P., van Ommen, T.: Inconsistency of Bayesian inference for misspecified linear models, and a proposal for repairing it. Bayesian Anal. **12**(4), 1069–1103 (2017)
17. Huber, P.J., Ronchetti, E.M.: Robust Statistics. Wiley Series in Probability and Statistics, 2nd edn. Wiley, Hoboken (2009)
18. Hüllermeier, E., Waegeman, W.: Aleatoric and epistemic uncertainty in machine learning: an introduction to concepts and methods. Mach. Learn. **3**(110), 457–506 (2021)
19. Kapoor, S., Maddox, W.J., Izmailov, P., Wilson, A.G.: On uncertainty, tempering, and data augmentation in Bayesian classification. In: Koyejo, S., Mohamed, S., Agarwal, A., Belgrave, D., Cho, K., Oh, A. (eds.) Advances in Neural Information Processing Systems, vol. 35, pp. 18211–18225. Curran Associates, Inc. (2022). https://proceedings.neurips.cc/paper_files/paper/2022/file/73e018a0123b35a3e64269526f9096c9-Paper-Conference.pdf
20. Kendall, A., Gal, Y.: What uncertainties do we need in Bayesian deep learning for computer vision? In: Advances in Neural Information Processing Systems, vol. 30 (2017)
21. Klibanoff, P., Hanany, E.: Updating preferences with multiple priors. Theor. Econ. **2**(3), 261–298 (2007)
22. Marinacci, M., Montrucchio, L.: Introduction to the mathematics of ambiguity. In: Gilboa, I. (ed.) Uncertainty in Economic Theory: A Collection of Essays in Honor of David Schmeidler's 65th Birthday. Routledge, London (2004)

23. Rakovi, S.V., Levine, W.S.: Handbook of Model Predictive Control, 1st edn. Birkhäuser, Basel (2018)

24. Rudin, W.: Principles of Mathematical Analysis, 3rd edn. McGraw-Hill, New York (1976)

25. Sale, Y., Caprio, M., Hüllermeier, E.: Is the volume of a credal set a good measure for epistemic uncertainty? In: Evans, R.J., Shpitser, I. (eds.) Proceedings of the Thirty-Ninth Conference on Uncertainty in Artificial Intelligence. Proceedings of Machine Learning Research, vol. 216, pp. 1795–1804. PMLR (2023)

26. Smith, L., Gal, Y.: Understanding measures of uncertainty for adversarial example detection. arXiv preprint arXiv:1803.08533 (2018)

27. Troffaes, M.C., de Cooman, G.: Lower Previsions. Wiley, Chichester (2014)

28. Walley, P.: Coherent lower (and upper) probabilities. Technical report, University of Warwick, Coventry (1981)

29. Walley, P.: Statistical Reasoning with Imprecise Probabilities, Monographs on Statistics and Applied Probability, vol. 42. Chapman and Hall, London (1991)

30. Wasserman, L.A., Kadane, J.B.: Bayes' theorem for Choquet capacities. Ann. Stat. **18**(3), 1328–1339 (1990)

31. Wimmer, L., Sale, Y., Hofman, P., Bischl, B., Hüllermeier, E.: Quantifying aleatoric and epistemic uncertainty in machine learning: are conditional entropy and mutual information appropriate measures? In: Evans, R.J., Shpitser, I. (eds.) Proceedings of the Thirty-Ninth Conference on Uncertainty in Artificial Intelligence. Proceedings of Machine Learning Research, vol. 216, pp. 2282–2292. PMLR (2023)

Deep Learning and MCMC with aggVAE for Shifting Administrative Boundaries: Mapping Malaria Prevalence in Kenya

Elizaveta Semenova[1,6]([✉]) [iD], Swapnil Mishra[2,7] [iD], Samir Bhatt[3,4,8] [iD],
Seth Flaxman[1,6] [iD], and H Juliette T Unwin[4,5,9]([✉]) [iD]

[1] Department of Computer Science, University of Oxford, Oxford, UK
`elizaveta.p.semenova@gmail.com`, `seth.flaxman@cs.ox.ac.uk`
[2] Saw Swee Hock School of Public Health and Institute of Data Science, National
University of Singapore and NUHS, Singapore, Singapore
`swapnil.mishra@nus.edu.sg`
[3] School of Public Health, University of Copenhagen, Copenhagen, Denmark
`samir.bhatt@sund.ku.dk`
[4] School of Public Health, Imperial College London, London, UK
[5] School of Mathematics, University of Bristol, Bristol, UK
`juliette.unwin@bristol.ac.uk`
[6] Machine Learning and Global Health Network, Oxford, UK
[7] Machine Learning and Global Health Network, Singapore, UK
[8] Machine Learning and Global Health Network, Copenhagen, London, UK
[9] Machine Learning and Global Health Network, Bristol, UK
`http://www.MLGH.net`

Abstract. Model-based disease mapping remains a fundamental policy-informing tool in the fields of public health and disease surveillance. Hierarchical Bayesian models have emerged as the state-of-the-art approach for disease mapping since they are able to both capture structure in the data and robustly characterise uncertainty. When working with areal data, e.g. aggregates at the administrative unit level such as district or province, current models rely on the adjacency structure of areal units to account for spatial correlations and perform shrinkage. The goal of disease surveillance systems is to track disease outcomes over time. This task is especially challenging in crisis situations which often lead to redrawn administrative boundaries, meaning that data collected before and after the crisis are no longer directly comparable. Moreover, the adjacency-based approach ignores the continuous nature of spatial processes and cannot solve the change-of-support problem, i.e. when estimates are required to be produced at different administrative levels or levels of aggregation. We present a novel, practical, and easy to implement solution to solve these problems relying on a methodology combining deep generative modelling and fully Bayesian inference: we build on the recently proposed PriorVAE method able to encode spatial priors over small areas with variational autoencoders by encoding aggregates over administrative units. We map malaria prevalence in Kenya, a country in which administrative boundaries changed in 2010.

© The Author(s), under exclusive license to Springer Nature Switzerland AG 2024
F. Cuzzolin and M. Sultana (Eds.): Epi UAI 2023, LNAI 14523, pp. 13–27, 2024.
https://doi.org/10.1007/978-3-031-57963-9_2

Keywords: MCMC · VAE · disease mapping

1 Introduction

Malaria is one of the major causes of mortality in sub-Saharan Africa, with a disproportionate burden on young children. In Kenya, a country with a long history of malaria control, approximately 75% of the population was still at risk in 2022 (U.S. President's Malaria Initiative, 2022). As malaria control programs continue to create novel control strategies, district-level disease mapping remains a fundamental surveillance tool for analysing the present and historical distribution of the disease in both space and time. However, disease tracking becomes more difficult in the situation of crises. For example, political factors have historically driven decentralisation across developing countries often leading to changes in administrative boundaries. Many of countries have increased their number of sub-national administrative units, including more than twenty countries in sub-Saharan Africa (Hassan, 2016). Some countries have experienced multiple changes of boundaries, such as Kenya. Methodologically, district-level disease mapping in Kenya can be challenging because administrative boundaries changed in 2010: while the old system consisted of 8 provinces and 69 districts (Fig. 1, left), the new system contains 47 districts (Fig. 1, middle) which do not coincide with the old boundaries. This change is hard to tackle with standard disease mapping tools.

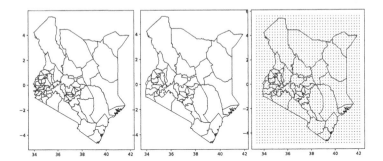

Fig. 1. Map of Kenya with district borders before 2010 (left), district borders from 2010 (middle), and computational grid used (right).

Hierarchical Bayesian models are the state-of-the-art approach for disease mapping (MacNab, 2022, Kang et al., 2016, Wakefield et al., 2000) since they are able to capture structure in the data, as well as to characterise uncertainty. Modern literature builds on a series of foundational works by Besag (1974), Clayton (1992), Bernardinelli and Montomoli (1992), Bernadinelli et al. (1997), Clayton et al. (1993) who instigated a paradigm shift from the frequentist to the Bayesian approach in disease mapping. Bayesian disease mapping since the

1980s and 1990s has Bayesian hierarchical models as its foundation, with no shortage of examples in malaria mapping (Gemperli et al., 2006, Gosoniu et al., 2006, Hay et al., 2009, Reid et al., 2010, Bhatt et al., 2015, 2017, Snow et al., 2017, Weiss et al., 2019). Markov chain Monte Carlo (MCMC) simulation methods, especially as implemented in probabilistic programming languages like BUGS and Stan, are a common approach to estimation, learning, and inference of unknown quantities and parameters. In recent years approximate inference algorithms, such as integrated nested Laplace approximation (INLA) have gained popularity (Martins et al., 2013). While such tools provide convenient interfaces to a set of predefined (and well documented) models, they do not provide as much flexibility for custom model development as probabilistic programming languages. This limits their applicability to specific classes of applied research, including the problem of aggregation and change-of-support which we study here. MCMC, on the contrary, is a general sampling technique for sampling from a possibly unnormalised target density $\pi(z)$, i.e. the posterior (Robert et al., 1999, Gelman et al., 1995).

MCMC is a computational method that generates a sequence of samples from a target distribution by constructing a specific kind of Markov chain that is guaranteed to converge to the target distribution asymptotically. In practice, MCMC sampling is performed for a finite number of iterations N, where N is sufficiently large for MCMC to converge. MCMC convergence and efficiency can be assessed via diagnostic tools, such as the $\hat{R}$ statistic and effective sample size (ESS) metrics, respectively (Vehtari et al., 2021). The $\hat{R}$ statistic, also known as the potential scale reduction factor, is a measure used to assess the convergence of multiple MCMC chains by comparing the within-chain variance to the between-chain variance. The ESS statistic quantifies the amount of independent information obtained from the generated samples, reflecting the effective size of the sample in terms of capturing the true underlying distribution. The critically important property of MCMC is that in the asymptotic limit, it guarantees *exact* samples from the target density. In health policy-related applications where modelling informs decision-making this property makes MCMC preferable to non-exact methods (such as variational Bayes). However, MCMC scales poorly for problems involving correlation structures, such as Gaussian Processes (GPs). Additional issues inherent to MCMC are autocorrelation in the produced samples, meaning that chains must be simulated for a prohibitively long time in order to obtain reliable uncertainty estimates. It is highly desirable for disease mapping models to retain modelling flexibility and reliability of MCMC, and, at the same time, to improve inference speed and efficiency.

The main modelling tool for capturing spatial correlation in a disease mapping model is the Gaussian process (GP) prior, whose realisation over a finite number of points is a multivariate Normal ($\mathcal{MVN}$) distribution. The most common type of spatial data analysed in this context is *areal* data, i.e. data obtained via aggregation of individual observations over spatial areas, such as administrative units. Statistical models describing areal data typically rely on the adjacency structure of areal units to account for spatial correlation. One drawback of this approach is that it disregards the continuous nature of underlying processes and potential heterogeneity within each region, especially large ones. Additionally, adjacency-based methods are very rigid with respect to the change-of-support problem, i.e. when administrative boundaries change or when mapping needs to be done at a different administrative level. The spatial aggregation process has been proposed in the literature to address this issue: an observational model is designed using the integration of the GP over the corresponding region (Tanaka et al., 2019, Yousefi et al., 2019, Zhu et al., 2021, Johnson et al., 2019).

In this work, we present a novel, practical and easy to implement solution of the change-of-support problem relying on a methodology combining deep generative modelling and fully Bayesian inference. Our approach is twofold:

- We view the spatial process as continuous. Rather than performing modelling based on the adjacency structure, we model the latent GP process on a fine spatial scale over an artificial computational grid covering the domain of interest and obtain unit-level estimates via aggregation. This approach has been used before in order to better capture continuity than adjacency-based methods.
- We extend the recently proposed PriorVAE (Semenova et al., 2022) method of encoding spatial priors with variational autoencoders to the change-of-support problem and malaria prevalence mapping in Kenya. Realisations of GP priors are generated on the fine spatial grid, and then aggregated to the level of administrative units. The aggregated values are encoded using the PriorVAE technique. The trained priors, termed aggVAE, are then used at the MCMC inference stage instead of combining the generation of GP priors and the aggregation step at each MCMC iteration.

We show that MCMC using the aggVAE approximate prior is faster and more efficient within an MCMC inference scheme than MCMC relying on the exact GP prior.

Our paper is structured as follows: in Sect. 2.1 we describe models from classical spatial statistics used to analyse areal data. In Sect. 2.2 we introduce the field of deep generative modelling and in particular the VAE architecture. In Sect. 2.3 we summarise the PriorVAE method of encoding spatial priors. In Sect. 3 we propose the aggVAE method allowing to encode aggregated latent GP evaluations. Our application to malaria prevalence mapping in Kenya is presented in Sect. 4 and we conclude by discussing limitations and future work in Sect. 5.

2 Background

2.1 Spatial Statistics Models of Areal Data

Classical statistical models describing areal data typically rely on the adjacency structure of areal units to account for spatial correlation, that is, nearby regions will likely be similar to each other. The prior on the spatial term in such models can be written as

$$f \sim \mathcal{MVN}(0, Q^{-1}),$$

where Q denotes the inverse covariance or precision matrix. Adjacency characterises the neighborhood structure allowing to calculate Q based on the connectedness of the adjacency graph. These methods take advantage of the tendency for neighboring areas to possess similar features. Besag (1974) first proposed the Conditional Auto-Regressive (CAR) with

$$Q = \tau(I - \alpha A),$$

where τ denotes the marginal precision, A is the adjacency matrix and α is a parameter capturing the amount of spatial dependence. Variations of this model were later proposed and include intrinsic CAR (iCAR): (Besag et al., 1991)

$$Q = \tau(D - A),$$

where D is the diagonal matrix consisting of the total number of neighbours for each area, proper CAR (pCAR) (Cressie, 2015) with

$$Q = \tau(D - \alpha A),$$

Leroux CAR (LCAR) (Leroux et al., 2000) with

$$Q = \tau(\alpha(D - A) + (1 - \alpha)I),$$

Besag-York-Mollié (BYM) model (Besag et al., 1991):

$$Q = \frac{1}{\tau_s}(D - A) + \frac{1}{\tau_{\text{iid}}}I,$$

BYM2 (Riebler et al., 2016).

2.2   Variational Autoencoders (VAEs)

A Variational Autoencoder (VAE) is a type of generative model that uses deep learning techniques to generate new data samples $\hat{y} \in \mathcal{Y} \subset \mathbb{R}^n$ that resemble the original training data $y \in \mathcal{Y}$. It consists of two parts: an encoder $E_\phi(.)$ that maps input data to a lower-dimensional representation (latent space) $\mathcal{Z} \subset \mathbb{R}^d, \quad d < n$, and a decoder $D_\psi(.)$ that maps the latent representation $z \in \mathcal{Z}$ back to the original data space. The encoder and decoder are trained together to minimise a reconstruction loss, which measures the difference between the original data and its reconstructed version. Additionally, a constraint is imposed on the latent representation to follow a prior distribution $q(z|y)$, such as a Gaussian distribution, allowing the model to generate new, unseen data by sampling from the prior and passing it through the decoder. Following Kingma and Welling (2013), the optimal parameters for the encoder and decoder are found by maximising the evidence lower bound, or, equivalently, minimising the loss:

$$\mathcal{L}_{\text{VAE}} = \mathbb{E}_{q(z|y)}\left[-\log p(y|z)\right] + KL\left[q(z|y)||p(z)\right].$$

The prior of the latent space and the variational distribution are typically chosen to have Gaussian forms: $p(z) = \mathcal{N}(0, I_d), \quad q(z|y) = \mathcal{N}(\mu_z, \sigma_z^2 I_d)$.

Fig. 2. Attribution of grid points over polygons (districts) before 2010 (left), and after 2010 (right). Grey points correspond to points falling outside of the country's borders, and points falling within the same polygon are represented with the same color. (Color figure online)

2.3 Encoding Spatial Priors with VAEs

πVAE (Mishra et al., 2022) and PriorVAE (Semenova et al., 2022) are two related VAE-based methods that can respectively encode continuous stochastic processes and their finite realisations. They utilize a trained decoder to approximate computationally complex GPs and $\mathcal{MVN}$s for Bayesian inference with MCMC, preserving the rigour of MCMC while ensuring scalability through the simplicity of the VAE's latent space. The key difference between the two methods is the type of prior they encode and the method of encoding: πVAE uses a low-dimensional embedding of function classes via a combination of a trainable feature mapping and a generative model, while PriorVAE directly encodes fixed, finite-dimensional GP realisations. In this work we will follow the PriorVAE approach. The method has been proposed as a scalable solution to the small area estimation (SAE) problem in spatial statistics as it encodes realisations of priors presented in Sect. 2.1. A characteristic property of PriorVAE is that it needs to be trained on a predefined spatial structure. On one hand, this is a disadvantage compared to πVAE since PriorVAE is unable to make predictions on off-grid locations. On the other hand, in the settings when the spatial structure is known in advance, PriorVAE is preferred due to its simpler computational setup, as only the prior-encoding VAE needs to be trained, without the need for learning of the feature map. The inference workflow using the PriorVAE method can be described as follows:

- Fix the spatial structure of interest $\{x_1, \ldots, x_n\}$ - a set of administrative units, or an artificial computational grid.
- Draw evaluations of a GP prior $\mathcal{GP}(.)$ over the spatial structure and use the vector of realisations

$$f_{\mathrm{GP}} = (f(x_1), \ldots, f(x_n))^T$$

as data for a VAE to encode.

- Train a VAE on the generated data to obtain the decoder $D_\psi(.)$.
- Perform Bayesian inference of the overarching model using MCMC, where f_{GP} is approximated by the trained decoder $D_\psi(.)$:

$$f_{GP} \approx \hat{f}_{GP} = f_{PriorVAE} = D_\psi(z_d), \quad z_d \sim \mathcal{N}(0, I_d).$$

3   Encoding Aggregates of the Gaussian Process Prior: aggVAE

3.1   GP Evaluations over a Fine Scale Grid

We view the underlying process as continuous and approximate it by evaluating the GP on a fine spatial grid $G = \{g_1, ...g_n\}$ (Fig. 1 (right)) covering the domain of interest. The grid is regular and has been chosen to ensure that at least one point of the grid g_j lies within each administrative unit p_i. GP prior realisations $f(.)$ are drawn over the artificial grid G as a multivariate normal distribution with a covariance matrix following the RBF[1] kernel:

$$f = \begin{pmatrix} f_1 \\ \vdots \\ f_n \end{pmatrix} \sim \mathcal{MVN}(0, \Sigma), \quad \Sigma_{jk} = \sigma^2 \exp\left(-\frac{d_{jk}^2}{2l^2}\right)$$

where $f_j = f(g_j)$, $d_{jk} = ||g_j - g_k||$ and σ^2, l are hyperparameters of the Gaussian Process. For the hyperparameters we used $l \sim InvGamma(3, 3)$ and $\sigma \sim \mathcal{N}^+(0.05)$ priors.

3.2   Computing GP Aggregates over Polygons

As the next step, we aggregate GP evaluations to the district level. Each district is viewed as a polygon $p_i, i = 1, ..., K$, and the computation takes the form

$$f_{aggGP}^{p_i} = \int_{p_i} f(s)ds \approx c \sum_{g_j \in p_i} f_j = c\bar{f}_{aggGP}^{p_i}. \tag{1}$$

Here $\bar{f}_{aggGP}^{p_i} = \sum_{g_j \in p_i} f_j$ and we have used the midpoint quadrature rule. The constant $c = \Delta x \Delta y$ with Δx and Δy being step sizes of the grid along the x and y axes, respectively. We can, therefore, construct a vector where each entry represents a spatial random effect at a district p_i:

$$f_{aggGP} = \begin{pmatrix} f_{aggGP}^{p_1} \\ \vdots \\ f_{aggGP}^{p_K} \end{pmatrix} \in \mathbb{R}^K. \tag{2}$$

---

[1] Any kernel can be used. We use RBF only as an example.

In practice, we implement 1 via matrix multiplication. For this, we precompute matrix M consisting of K rows and n columns with binary entries M_{ji}, indicating whether point j lies within polygon i (see Figs. 2):

$$M_{ji} = I_{\{g_j \in p_i\}}, \quad j = 1, ..., K, \quad i = 1, ..., n.$$

Hence, M serves as a lookup table, and if f is a vector of GP draws over the grid, the product Mf gives the vector of sums

$$\bar{f}_{\text{aggGP}} = Mf = \begin{pmatrix} \bar{f}^{p_1}_{\text{aggGP}} \\ \vdots \\ \bar{f}^{p_K}_{\text{aggGP}} \end{pmatrix} \tag{3}$$

This procedure can be performed both with respect to the old and new boundaries to obtain vectors $f^{\text{old}}_{\text{aggGP}}$ and $f^{\text{new}}_{\text{aggGP}}$, respectively, using M^{old} and M^{new} precomputed matrices.

3.3 Encoding GP Aggregates

In order to tackle the change-of-support problem, we encode $\bar{f}^{\text{old}}_{\text{aggGP}}$ and $\bar{f}^{\text{new}}_{\text{aggGP}}$ jointly. We construct a vector of dimension $K_1 + K_2$ of the form

$$\bar{f}^{\text{joint}}_{\text{aggGP}} = \begin{pmatrix} \bar{f}^{p_1^{\text{old}}}_{\text{aggGP}} \\ \cdots \\ \bar{f}^{p_{K_1}^{\text{old}}}_{\text{aggGP}} \\ ---- \\ \bar{f}^{p_1^{\text{new}}}_{\text{aggGP}} \\ \bar{f}^{p_{K_2}^{\text{new}}}_{\text{aggGP}} \end{pmatrix} = \begin{pmatrix} M^{\text{old}} f \\ M^{\text{new}} f \end{pmatrix} \in \mathbb{R}^{K_1 + K_2}.$$

and apply the PriorVAE method to $\bar{f}^{\text{joint}}_{\text{aggGP}}$, i.e. we encode GP aggregates jointly for old and new boundaries with a VAE using a lower-dimensional representation with independent standard Gaussian components $z_1, ..., z_d$, $d < K_1 + K_2$, $z_i \sim N(0, 1)$. We denote the new prior of the area-level spatial effect as f_{aggVAE}. This one-step prior can be used at the inference stage instead of the two step procedure where first evaluation $f_1, ..., f_n$ need to be drawn and then aggregated to obtain f_{aggGP}. We summarise the encoding and MCMC inference procedure using aggVAE in Algorithm 1.

4 Inference Using aggVAE: Mapping Malaria Prevalence in Kenya

Malaria prevalence is routinely mapped using disease surveillance data which was collected, for example, via the DHS programme. A number of survey clusters (households) are selected and individuals within a cluster get tested for the

- Fix spatial structure of areal units as a collection of polygons $P = \{p_1, \ldots, p_K\}$.
- Create an aritificial computational grid of sufficient granularity $G = \{g_1, \ldots, g_n\}$.
- Precompute the matrix of indicators M, $\quad M_{ji} = I_{\{g_j \subset p_i\}}$.
- Draw GP evaluations over G using a selected kernel $k(.,.)$: $f = (f_1, \ldots f_n)^T$.
- Compute GP aggregates at the level of P: $f_{\text{aggGP}} = cMf$
- Train PriorVAE on f_{aggGP} (or $\bar{f}_{\text{aggGP}}$) draws to obtain f_{aggVAE} priors
- Use f_{aggVAE} at inference within MCMC.

Algorithm 1: Inference procedure using aggVAE

presence or absence of malaria parasite. Malaria prevalence can then be modelled as the probability of a positive test among all tests. In this work we use results of the survey conducted in 2015. In 2010 administrative boundaries in Kenya changed (Fig. 1). We treat the 2015 data as static, i.e. we assume that the same data was collected once before 2010 and once after 2010 by overlaying it with old and new boundaries. District-specific malaria prevalence $\theta_i, i \in 1, \ldots K$ is inferred using the Binomial distribution

$$\begin{cases} n_i^{\text{pos}} & \sim \text{Bin}(n_i^{\text{tests}}, \theta_i), \\ \text{logit}(\theta_i) & = b_0 + f_{\text{aggGP}}^{p_i}. \end{cases} \qquad (4)$$

where n_i^{tests} and n_i^{pos} are the number of total and positive RDT tests observed in district i, correspondingly. $f_{\text{aggGP}}^{p_i}$ in 4 is the two-step spatial prior requiring first the sampling of the GP draws and the subsequent aggregation step. To avoid this procedure, we approximate $f_{\text{aggGP}}^{p_i}$ with $f_{\text{aggVAE}}^{p_i}$ and use the following model for inference:

$$\begin{cases} n_i^{\text{pos}} & \sim \text{Bin}(n_i^{\text{tests}}, \theta_i), \\ \text{logit}(\theta_i) & = b_0 + s f_{\text{aggVAE}}^{p_i}. \end{cases} \qquad (5)$$

The additional parameter s is introduced here to account for us encoding $\bar{f}_{\text{aggGP}}$ rather than f_{aggGP}, as well as to prevent our VAEs from oversmoothing; the additional parameter can correct for that at the inference stage.

Our goal is to compare speed and efficiency in terms of effective sample sizes (ESS) of MCMC inference using models described in 4 and 5. Both inference models were implemented using the Numpyro probabilistic programming language (Phan et al., 2019, Bingham et al., 2019) and the encoding of aggVAE was performed using the JAX library (Bradbury et al., 2018). We ran both MCMC inference models using 200 warm-up and 1000 posterior samples. Results of the comparison are presented in Table 1. The model using aggGP prior ran 10K times longer, and after 14h has not fully converged. After 1200 total iterations it has only achieved $\hat{R} = 1.4$. Traceplots and posterior distributions for the GP lengthscale and variance parameter are presented on Figs. 3 and 4, correspondingly. When comparing spatial random effects (REs) corresponding to old and new boundaries, aggGP model particularly struggles with the old ones: maximum Gelman-Rubin statistic is $\hat{R} = 1.10$ for REs over the old boundaries, and $\hat{R} = 1.06$ for RFs over the new boundaries. Graphical comparison of the crude estimates, i.e. observed crude prevalence ($\theta_{\text{crude}} = \frac{n_i^{\text{pos}}}{n_i^{\text{tests}}}$) and estimates obtained by the aggGP and aggVAE models are presented on Figs. 5 and 6, correspondingly. Maps of crude prevalence estimates, estimates obtained by the aggGP and aggVAE models are presented on Fig. 7 for boundaries before 2010 and on Fig. 8 for boundaries from 2010.

Table 1. Comparison of MCMC for models with f_{aggGP} and f_{aggVAE} spatial random effects (REs) using 200 warm-up and 1000 steps

Model (used prior)	aggGP RE	aggVAE RE
Elapsed time	14h[a]	8 s
Average ESS of the REs	129	231
ESS per minute	0.15	1732
Maximum $\hat{R}$ of REs, boundaries before 2010	1.10	1.01
Maximum $\hat{R}$ of REs, boundaries from 2010	1.07	1.01
Average ESS of the REs, boundaries from 2010	132	222
Average ESS of the REs, boundaries from 2010	125	245

[a] After this time aggGP model has not fully converged; e.g. the Gelamn-Rubin statistic for the lengthc-sale parameter is $\hat{R} = 1.4$.

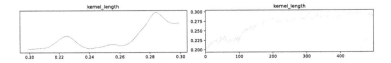

Fig. 3. Posterior distribution (left) and traceplot (right) of the GP lengthscale parameter.

5   Discussion and Future Work

In this work we have demonstrated the applicability of aggregated GP priors to represent spatial random effect instead of traditional adjacency-based models, and presented a scalable solution to the change-of-support problem by jointly encoding GP aggregates using the PriorVAE technique. Modelling on fine resolution scales is attractive since this approach allows us to capture continuity,

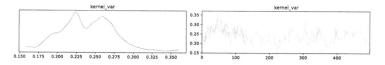

Fig. 4. Posterior distribution (left) and traceplot (right) of the GP variance parameter.

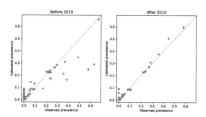

Fig. 5. Observed and estimated prevalence produced by the aggGP model. The model has not converged after 1200 MCMC steps and particularly struggles with estimates over the old bounaries.

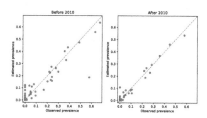

Fig. 6. Observed and estimated prevalence produced by the aggVAE model.

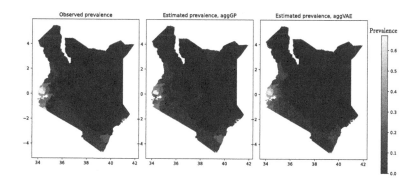

Fig. 7. Map of malaria prevalence in Kenya based on district boundaries before 2010: (a) crude prevalence estimates, (b) estimates obtained by the aggGP model, and (c) estimates obtained by the aggVAE model.

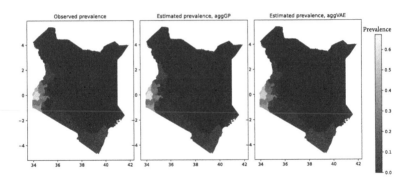

Fig. 8. Map of malaria prevalence in Kenya based on district boundaries after 2010: (a) crude prevalence estimates, (b) estimates obtained by the aggGP model, and (c) estimates obtained by the aggVAE model.

but it is computationally cumbersome. By introducing the aggVAE prior, we alleviate the computational difficulties. Our results showed that inference using aggVAE priors is orders of magnitude faster and more efficient than inference performed using the GP priors; effective sample size per second is thousands times higher when using aggVAE prior than combining the original GP priors and the aggregation step to obtain aggGP. Our work lays foundation for future extensions allowing to capture heterogeneity of continuous covariates X, such as environmental factors, at a fine spatial scale, by including them into the linear predictor of the model as the fixed effect term: $b_0 + X\beta + f$. We used the RBF kernel to model GP on the fine spatial scale. This kernel defines smooth and stationary GP draws. However, the presented methodology is kernel-agnostic, and any other kernel can be used instead, including non-stationary kernels. One drawback of the PriorVAE method is pertinent in the current work as well: aggVAE is not explicitly encoding hyperparameters of the GP, such as length-scale, and, hence, is not able to infer them. Future extensions should focus on closing this gap, e.g. conditional variational autoencoders can be used instead to overcome this issue (Semenova et al., 2023). Since aggVAE provides a prior that does not have a closed form solution but is rather obtained in an empirical way by training a neural work, theoretical properties of such priors and their influence on downstream inference should be studied in more detail.While modelling prevalence, we have taken the number of positive and negative tests at their face values. Sensitivity of the test, however, may play a role. We also treated survey locations as noise-free, while due to privacy they have 10 km precision. Both facts should be taken into account while performing modelling for real-life applications and constitute future work.

Acknowledgments. E.S. acknowledges supported in part by the AI2050 program at Schmidt Futures (Grant [G-22-64476]). S.F. and E.S. acknowledge the EPSRC (EP/V002910/2). SM acknowledges support from the National Research Foundation via The NRF Fellowship Class of 2023 Award (NRF-NRFF15-2023-0010). H.J.T.U acknowledges funding from the MRC Centre for Global Infectious Disease Analysis (reference MR/X020258/1), funded by the UK Medical Research Council (MRC). This UK funded award is carried out in the frame of the Global Health EDCTP3 Joint Undertaking. S.B. acknowledges funding from the MRC Centre for Global Infectious Disease Analysis (reference MR/X020258/1), funded by the UK Medical Research Council (MRC). This UK funded award is carried out in the frame of the Global Health EDCTP3 Joint Undertaking. S.B. acknowledges support from the National Institute for Health and Care Research (NIHR) via the Health Protection Research Unit in Modelling and Health Economics, which is a partnership between the UK Health Security Agency (UKHSA), Imperial College London, and the London School of Hygiene & Tropical Medicine (grant code NIHR200908). (The views expressed are those of the authors and not necessarily those of the UK Department of Health and Social Care, NIHR, or UKHSA.). S.B. acknowledges support from the Novo Nordisk Foundation via The Novo Nordisk Young Investigator Award (NNF20OC0059309). SB acknowledges the Danish National Research Foundation (DNRF160) through the chair grant. S.B. acknowledges support from The Eric and Wendy Schmidt Fund For Strategic Innovation via the Schmidt Polymath Award (G-22-63345).

Data and Code Availability. Data containing administrative boundaries of Kenya are publicly available: current boundaries (https://data.humdata.org/dataset/ 2c0b7571-4bef-4347-9b81-b2174c13f9ef/resource/03df9cbb- 0b4f-4f22-9eb7-3cbd0157fd3d/download/ken_adm_iebc_20191031_shp.zip) and old boundaries (https://www.wri.org/data/kenya-gis-data) can be freely downloaded. Malaria prevalence data was obtained from DHS 2015 survey and contains information on locations of clusters and test positivity to calculate district-specific prevalence; it can be requested from the DHS programme (https://dhsprogram.com/). Code to reproduce the results is available at https://github.com/MLGlobalHealth/aggVAE.

Disclosure of Interests. Authors do not have any competing interests to declare. Any opinions, findings and conclusions or recommendations expressed in this material are those of the author(s) and do not reflect the views of the National Research Foundation, Singapore

References

Bernadinelli, L., Pascutto, C., Best, N.G., Gilks, W.R.: Disease mapping with errors in covariates. Stat. Med. **16**(7), 741–752 (1997)

Bernardinelli, L., Montomoli, C.: Empirical Bayes versus fully Bayesian analysis of geographical variation in disease risk. Stat. Med. **11**(8), 983–1007 (1992)

Besag, J.: Spatial interaction and the statistical analysis of lattice systems. J. Roy. Stat. Soc.: Ser. B (Methodol.) **36**(2), 192–225 (1974)

Besag, J., York, J., Mollié, A.: Bayesian image restoration, with two applications in spatial statistics. Ann. Inst. Stat. Math. **43**, 1–20 (1991)

Bhatt, S., et al.: The effect of malaria control on *Plasmodium falciparum* in Africa between 2000 and 2015. Nature **526**(7572), 207–211 (2015)

Bhatt, S., Cameron, E., Flaxman, S.R., Weiss, D.J., Smith, D.L., Gething, P.W.: Improved prediction accuracy for disease risk mapping using gaussian process stacked generalization. J. Roy. Soc. Interface **14**(134), 20170520 (2017)

Bingham, E., et al.: Pyro: deep universal probabilistic programming. J. Mach. Learn. Res. **20**, 28:1–28:6 (2019). http://jmlr.org/papers/v20/18-403.html

Bradbury, J., et al.: JAX: composable transformations of Python+NumPy programs (2018). http://github.com/google/jax

Clayton, D.G.: Bayesian methods for mapping disease risk. In: Geographical and Environmental Epidemiology: Methods for Small-Area Studies, pp. 205–220 (1992)

Clayton, D.G., Bernardinelli, L., Montomoli, C.: Spatial correlation in ecological analysis. Int. J. Epidemiol. **22**(6), 1193–1202 (1993)

Cressie, N.: Statistics for Spatial Data. Wiley, Hoboken (2015)

Gelman, A., Carlin, J.B., Stern, H.S., Rubin, D.B.: Bayesian Data Analysis. Chapman and Hall/CRC (1995)

Gemperli, A., et al.: Mapping malaria transmission in West and Central Africa. Trop. Med. Int. Health **11**(7), 1032–1046 (2006)

Gosoniu, L., Vounatsou, P., Sogoba, N., Smith, T.: Bayesian modelling of geostatistical malaria risk data. Geospat. Health **1**(1), 127–139 (2006)

Hassan, M.: A state of change: district creation in Kenya after the beginning of multiparty elections. Polit. Res. Q. **69**(3), 510–521 (2016)

Hay, S.I., et al.: A world malaria map: plasmodium falciparum endemicity in 2007. PLoS Med. **6**(3), e1000048 (2009)

Johnson, O., Diggle, P., Giorgi, E.: A spatially discrete approximation to log-Gaussian Cox processes for modelling aggregated disease count data. Stat. Med. **38**(24), 4871–4887 (2019)

Kang, S.Y., Cramb, S.M., White, N.M., Ball, S.J., Mengersen, K.L.: Making the most of spatial information in health: a tutorial in Bayesian disease mapping for areal data. Geospat. Health **11**(2), 190–198 (2016)

Kingma, D.P., Welling, M.: Auto-encoding variational bayes. arXiv preprint arXiv:1312.6114 (2013)

Leroux, B.G., Lei, X., Breslow, N.: Estimation of disease rates in small areas: a new mixed model for spatial dependence. In: Halloran, M.E., Berry, D. (eds.) Statistical Models in Epidemiology, the Environment, and Clinical Trials. IMA, vol. 116, pp. 179–191. Springer, New York (2000). https://doi.org/10.1007/978-1-4612-1284-3_4

MacNab, Y.C.: Bayesian disease mapping: past, present, and future. Spatial Stat. **50**, 100593 (2022)

Martins, T.G., Simpson, D., Lindgren, F., Rue, H.: Bayesian computing with INLA: new features. Comput. Stat. Data Anal. **67**, 68–83 (2013)

Mishra, S., Flaxman, S., Berah, T., Pakkanen, M., Zhu, H., Bhatt, S.: piVAE: encoding stochastic process priors with variational autoencoders. Stat. Comput. (2022)

Phan, D., Pradhan, N., Jankowiak, M.: Composable effects for flexible and accelerated probabilistic programming in NumPyro. arXiv preprint arXiv:1912.11554 (2019)

Reid, H., et al.: Mapping malaria risk in Bangladesh using Bayesian geostatistical models. Am. J. Trop. Med. Hyg. **83**(4), 861 (2010)

Riebler, A., Sørbye, S.H., Simpson, D., Rue, H.: An intuitive Bayesian spatial model for disease mapping that accounts for scaling. Stat. Methods Med. Res. **25**(4), 1145–1165 (2016)

Robert, C.P., Casella, G., Casella, G.: Monte Carlo Statistical Methods, vol. 2. Springer, New York (1999). https://doi.org/10.1007/978-1-4757-4145-2

Semenova, E., et al.: PriorVAE: encoding spatial priors with variational autoencoders for small-area estimation. J. R. Soc. Interface **19**(191), 20220094 (2022)

Semenova, E., Verma, P., Cairney-Leeming, M., Solin, A., Bhatt, S., Flaxman, S.: PriorCVAE: scalable MCMC parameter inference with Bayesian deep generative modelling. arXiv preprint arXiv:2304.04307 (2023)

Snow, R.W., et al.: The prevalence of *Plasmodium falciparum* in sub-Saharan Africa since 1900. Nature **550**(7677), 515–518 (2017)

Tanaka, Y., et al.: Spatially aggregated gaussian processes with multivariate areal outputs. In: Advances in Neural Information Processing Systems, vol. 32 (2019)

U.S. President's Malaria Initiative. U.S. president's malaria initiative Kenya malaria operational plan FY 2022 (2022). www.pmi.gov

Vehtari, A., Gelman, A., Simpson, D., Carpenter, B., Bürkner, P.-C.: Rank-normalization, folding, and localization: an improved R for assessing convergence of MCMC (with discussion). Bayesian Anal. **16**(2), 667–718 (2021)

Wakefield, J.C., Best, N.G., Waller, L.: Bayesian approaches to disease mapping. In: Spatial Epidemiology: Methods and Applications, vol. 59 (2000)

Weiss, D.J., et al.: Mapping the global prevalence, incidence, and mortality of Plasmodium falciparum, 2000–17: a spatial and temporal modelling study. The Lancet **394**(10195), 322–331 (2019)

Yousefi, F., Smith, M.T., Alvarez, M.: Multi-task learning for aggregated data using Gaussian processes. In: Advances in Neural Information Processing Systems, vol. 32 (2019)

Zhu, H., et al.: Aggregated Gaussian processes with multiresolution earth observation covariates. arXiv preprint arXiv:2105.01460 (2021)

Bag of Policies for Distributional Deep Exploration

Asen Nachkov[1(✉)], Luchen Li[1], Giulia Luise[1], Filippo Valdettaro[1],
and A. Aldo Faisal[1,2]

[1] Brain and Behaviour Lab, Department of Computing, Imperial College London,
London SW7 2AZ, UK
a.t.nachkov@gmail.com, {filippo.valdettaro20,a.faisal}@imperial.ac.uk
[2] Chair in Digital Health and Data Science, University of Bayreuth,
95447 Bayreuth, Germany

Abstract. Efficient exploration in complex environments remains a major challenge for reinforcement learning (RL). Compared to previous Thompson sampling-inspired mechanisms that enable temporally extended exploration, i.e., deep exploration, we focus on deep exploration in distributional RL. We develop a general purpose approach, Bag of Policies (BoP), that can be built on top of any return distribution estimator by maintaining a population of its copies. BoP consists of an ensemble of multiple heads that are updated independently. During training, each episode is controlled by only one of the heads and the collected state-action pairs are used to update all heads off-policy, leading to distinct learning signals for each head which diversify learning and behaviour. To test whether optimistic ensemble method can improve on distributional RL as it does on scalar RL, we implement the BoP approach with a population of distributional actor-critics using Bayesian Distributional Policy Gradients (BDPG). The population thus approximates a posterior distribution of return distributions along with a posterior distribution of policies. Our setup allows to analyze global posterior uncertainty along with local curiosity bonus simultaneously for exploration. As BDPG is already an optimistic method, this pairing helps to investigate the extent to which accumulating curiosity bonuses is beneficial. Overall BoP results in greater robustness and speed during learning as demonstrated by our experimental results on ALE Atari games.

Keywords: Distributional RL · Exploration · Intrinsic motivation

1 Introduction

Distributional RL (DiRL) has rapidly established its place among reinforcement learning (RL) algorithms (Bellemare et al., 2017) as a powerful improvement over non-distributional value-based counterparts (Lyle et al., 2019). In DiRL, the agent does not learn a single summary statistic of the return for each state-action pair, but instead learns the whole return distribution. While this does lead

© The Author(s), under exclusive license to Springer Nature Switzerland AG 2024
F. Cuzzolin and M. Sultana (Eds.): Epi UAI 2023, LNAI 14523, pp. 28–43, 2024.
https://doi.org/10.1007/978-3-031-57963-9_3

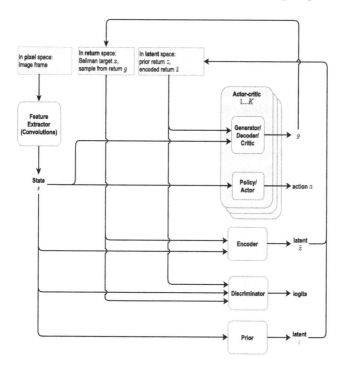

Fig. 1. Schematic and data flow in BoP.

to more stable learning and better performance (Lyle et al., 2019), it does not itself directly change the way actions are selected. In distributional extensions to value-based RL such as C51 (Bellemare et al., 2017) and QR-DQN (Dabney et al., 2018b), the agent still takes actions according to the mean of the estimated return distributions in each state-action pair. Thus, estimating a return distribution, at its core, provides performance advantages from better representation and evaluation which are unrelated to the action-selection and the exploration behaviour of the agent.

One of the major challenges in DiRL is to better leverage an estimated return distribution for action selection (Dabney et al., 2018a). In a discrete action setting, the agent could take the action maximizing the mean plus a time-dependent scaled standard deviation of the return (Mavrin et al., 2019). This approach, combined with computing the upper variance as an embodiment of the "optimism in the face of uncertainty" principle, has yielded considerable improvements in exploration. A DiRL solution based on Wasserstein-GAN (Freirich et al., 2019) captures uncertainty in the gradient magnitude of parameters. In the recent Bayesian Distributional Policy Gradients (BDPG) (Li and Faisal, 2021), a curiosity bonus in the form of information gain is added to the reward function, which motivates the agent to choose actions whose outcome has high epistemic uncertainty in terms of the return distribution estimation. These strategies all bias the data-collecting policy with a curiosity component computed from the return distribution modelling, instead of using only the mean returns as done in conventional RL.

In the meantime, one of the most effective exploration approaches centred around the idea of optimism in the face of uncertainty in scalar RL, are those based on posterior sampling or Thompson sampling (Thompson, 1935), as discussed in more detail in Sect. 3. These methods typically maintain an ensemble of randomized copies of the same function, relying on model diversity to select actions that are either relatively certainly optimal or uncertain, and therefore efficiently expand the data space with maximal information gathering.

In this work, we combine the ensemble method with already optimistic DiRL to assess whether the additional optimism from diversified model estimation is beneficial. To this end, we enhance BDPG (Li and Faisal, 2021) into multiple distributional actor-critic models to achieve a combination of both Thompson sampling and curiosity bonus-induced optimism. Crucially, we are now able to leverage the epistemic uncertainty of the agent in a two-pronged manner: First, through the Thompson sampling enabled by an ensemble of policies and return distributions (heads); Second, by using a local information gain inferred from the observed inaccuracies in each head's return distribution estimate.

Our contributions in this paper are as follows: we introduce the Bag of Policies framework, analyze its properties and the off-policy training aspects. We also explore variations of our algorithm and test its performance on the Atari Arcade Learning Environment (Bellemare et al., 2013). Our results suggest that Thompson sampling can indeed improve upon already optimistic DiRL. This finding is promising, as we now know that optimism can be accumulated in DiRL.

2   Preliminaries

A reinforcement learning (RL) task is modelled as a Markov decision process (MDP) $(\mathcal{S}, \mathcal{A}, \mathcal{R}, P, \gamma)$ (Puterman, 1994) where $\mathcal{S}$ is the set of possible states of the environment, $\mathcal{A}$ is the set of actions the agent can take, $\mathcal{R}$ is a reward function, P is the transition probability density for transitioning to a new state given the agent's current state and their selected action, and γ is the discount factor. States and actions can be continuous in our framework. The agent also learns or controls a possibly stochastic policy $\pi : \mathcal{S} \to P(\mathcal{A})$ mapping from states to a distribution over actions.

In our implementation the policy π is parameterized and updated with policy gradient (Sutton, 1999, Mnih et al., 2016, Schulman et al., 2016) to maximise an explicit objective function of the performance of the agent such as $\mathbb{E}_{s \sim d^{\pi}, a \sim \pi(\cdot|s)}[A(s,a) \log \pi(a|s)]$, where d^{π} is the stationary marginal state density induced by π and $A(s,a)$ is the advantage function.

The return for a given state $s \in \mathcal{S}$ is defined as the sum of discounted future rewards that the agent collects starting from the state s, $G^{\pi}(s) := \sum_{t=0}^{\infty} \gamma^t r_t$, $s_0 = s$. While we consider state-dependent return in this work, the idea also extends to action-dependent returns. The return is a random variable with potential aleatoric uncertainty (e.g. from stochastic state transitions). DiRL methods learn not only a single statistic of the return in a given state, but a representation of the whole distribution. Similar to the Bellman operator defined in conventional RL with respect to the mean of the return, one can use the distributional Bellman operator (Bellemare et al., 2017).

$$\mathcal{T}^\pi G^\pi(s) :\overset{D}{=} R(s) + \gamma G^\pi(s'), \tag{1}$$

where $R(s)$ is the random variable of the reward and $s' \sim P(\cdot|a,s), a \sim \pi(\cdot|s)$, to learn the state return distribution.

We test our idea of improving optimistic DiRL using (also optimistic) deep exploration on the DiRL method BDPG (Li and Faisal, 2021), as it provides an optimistic exploration bonus. BDPG interprets the distributional Bellman operator as a variational auto-encoding (VAE) process. It simultaneously minimizes a Wasserstein distance between the return distribution model and the distribution of the backup target, and performs joint-contrastive learning adversarially (Donahue et al. 2017) to force the encoder to approximate the posterior distribution over a latent variable induced by the decoder. Meanwhile, the VAE provides an estimate of information gain between samples from target and model return distributions, giving rise to the quantification of the epistemic uncertainty in return distribution modelling around the current state under the current policy. This information gain is then used to augment reward signals to encourage exploration. As an already (locally) optimistic DiRL method, BDPG is a good baseline to pair with Thompson sampling for our investigation of combining optimism in DiRL.

We introduce the superscript i in the notation π^i to denote the i-th policy in an ensemble of K distributional estimator actor-critic heads. Accordingly, A_t^i is the advantage of the i-th policy at timestep t. We adopt the notations used in BDPG to shorthand the model output state-return as $g(s) := G^\pi(s)$, and its Bellman backup target as $x(s) := \mathcal{T}^\pi G^\pi(s)$. They both belong to the return space. BDPG matches $g(s)$ to $x(s)$ in Wasserstein metric (under which the distributional Bellman operator is known to be a contraction (Bellemare et al., 2017)) with a deterministic decoder $p_\theta(x|z,s)$ that maps a latent random variable z to a return sample $g(s)$, a variational encoder $q_\phi(z|x,s)$ that approximates the posterior over z conditional on observed data $x(s)$, and a discriminator $D_\psi(x,z,s)$ to enforce joint-contrastive learning (Donahue et al. 2017). Algorithmic details are presented in the original paper (Li and Faisal, 2021). Dependency on s is omitted when no confusion is to be incurred. We adapt per-head shorthand from BDPG notations for the Bellman targets as x_t^i, the samples from the generators g_t^i, and latent variables for the generative process z_t^i.

3   Related Work

Closest to our work is the multi-worker or multi-head approaches which leverage Thompson sampling (Thompson, 1935) to diversify behaviour. Notice that unlike parallel approaches such as A3C (Mnih et al., 2016) and (variants Liang et al., 2018, Zhang et al., 2019) in which the multiple workers are updated with the same gradient, Thompson sampling allows the workers to learn from bootstrapped signals (Efron and Tibshirani, 1994) and to focus on where the current understanding is insufficient rather than merely cover more state space more quickly together than a single worker.

One early example of Thompson sampling in deep RL is the Bootstrapped DQN (Osband et al., 2016) which utilizes multiple Q-value "heads". Each head is initialized randomly and differently and then trained on their respective learning signal (with slightly different data or even identical data but distinct gradient). Thanks to this diversity, the heads' evaluations for a state-action pair tend to converge to the true value (which then allows the optimal action to be chosen) as the pair is being sufficiently visited. An action is then selected either because it is optimal or because its evaluation is uncertain, thus inducing optimistic action selection. This uncertainty is referred to as the epistemic uncertainty that would diminish as training data increases. Bootstrapped DQN and variants (Osband et al., 2019, Chen et al., 2017, O'Donoghue et al., 2018) can be thought of as representing a posterior distribution of the Q-function and thus give a measure of epistemic uncertainty in the Q-value estimation. Similarly, (Tang and Agrawal, 2020) approximates Thompson sampling by drawing network parameters for an RL model.

Ensemble method is important as it also allows for deep exploration by engaging the same policy for the duration of the whole episode. However, all ensemble-based exploration schemes for now are intended for conventional scalar RL, and the purpose of this work is to investigate whether deep exploration could improve performance in distributional RL, further still, whether the global optimism incurred by the ensemble effect can further enhance exploration efficiency when the agent is already optimistically biased on per-state basis. Combining ensemble technique with DiRL is not a trivial investigation and the benefit of diversity does not automatically propagate, as now we would be learning a posterior distribution over *distributions*, whilst admittedly the diversity over distributions is harder to maintain than that over numbers.

We base our approach on BDPG (Li and Faisal, 2021) which is a DiRL approach made up of a single distributional actor-critic and provides a local curiosity bonus favouring states whose return distribution estimations suffer from high epistemic uncertainty. BoP in contrast maintains a posterior distribution over return distributions and over policies, keeping track of both aleatoric and epistemic uncertainties about return distribution estimation simultaneously.

4   Bag of Policies (BoP)

In the following we lay out the structure, theory and variants of BoP. A schematic can be found in Fig. 1 and for the pseudocode please refer to Algorithm 1.

Algorithm 1. Bag of Policies

1: Initialize prior $p_\theta(z|s)$, encoder $q_\phi(z|x,s)$, discriminator $D_\psi(x,z,s)$, actor-critic population
   $\{G_\theta^i(z,s), \pi^i\}_{i=1}^K$
2: **while** not converged **do**
3:    // Roll-out stage
4:    training batch $\mathcal{D} \leftarrow \emptyset$
5:    Sample $k \sim \text{Uniform}(1, ..., K)$ // actor-critic to act
6:    **for** $t = 0$ to $T - 1$ **do**
7:       execute $a_t^k \sim \pi^k(\cdot|s_t)$, get r_t, s_{t+1}
8:       sample return $z_t \sim p_\theta(\cdot|s_t), g_t^i \leftarrow G_\theta^i(z_t, s_t), \ \forall i$
9:       $\mathcal{D} \leftarrow \mathcal{D} \cup \big(s_t, a_t, r_t, g_t^i, \log \pi^i(a_t|s_t)\big), \forall i$
10:    **end for**
11:    sample last return
   $z_T \sim p_\theta(\cdot|s_T), g_T^i \leftarrow G_\theta^i(z_T, s_T), \ \forall i$
12:    // Data-driven estimation stage
13:    **for** $t \in \mathcal{D}, \ \forall i$ **do**
14:       estimate off-policy advantage A_t^i
15:       compute Bellman target $x_t^i \leftarrow A_t^i + g_t^i$
16:       compute mixed curiosity reward
   $\hat{r}_t^i \propto \text{KL}\big(q_\phi(\cdot|x_t^k, s_t) \ || \ q_\phi(\cdot|g_t^i, s_t)\big)$
17:       augment A_t^i by replacing r_t with $r_t + \hat{r}_t^i$
18:    **end for**
19:    // Update stage
20:    // Train with minibatch $B \subset \mathcal{D}$
21:    **for** $t \in B$ **do**
22:       encode $\tilde{z}_t^i \sim q_\phi(\cdot|x_t^i, s_t), \ \forall i$
23:       sample adversaries
   $z_t^i \sim p_\theta(\cdot|s_t), \ \tilde{x}_t^i \leftarrow G_{\bar{\theta}}^i(z_t^i, s_t), \ \forall i$
24:       take averages
   $\bar{z}_t = \frac{1}{K}\sum_{i=1}^K \tilde{z}_t^i, \bar{x}_t = \frac{1}{K}\sum_{i=1}^K \tilde{x}_t^i$
25:    **end for**
26:    update D_ψ by ascending
   $\frac{1}{|B|}\sum_{t \in B}\big[\log D_\psi(\bar{x}_t, z_t, s_t) +$
                   $\log\big(1 - D_\psi(x_t, \bar{z}_t, s_t)\big)\big]$
27:    update encoder, prior by ascending
   $\frac{1}{|B|}\sum_{t \in B}\big[\log\big(1 - D_\psi(\bar{x}_t, z_t, s_t)\big) +$
                   $\log D_\psi(x_t, \bar{z}_t, s_t)\big]$
28:    update $G_\theta^i, \ \forall i$ by descending
   $\frac{1}{|B|}\sum_{t \in B}||x_t^i - G_\theta^i(\tilde{z}_t^i, s_t)||_2^2$
29:    update $\pi^i, \ \forall i$ by ascending
   $\frac{1}{|B|}\sum_{t \in B}\log \pi^i(a_t|s_t)A_t^i$
30: **end while**

4.1 Architecture

The Bag of Policies (BoP) framework can be applied to any DiRL estimator. In this work we have chosen BDPG (Li and Faisal, 2021) as the implementation

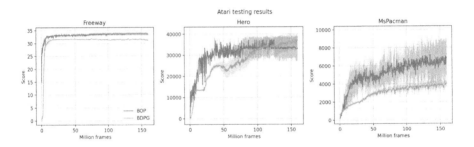

Fig. 2. Comparison of BDPG and BoP on selected Atari environments.

framework because, unlike other estimators (Bellemare et al. 2017, Dabney et al. 2018b), it further exploits local epistemic uncertainty. We rely on its architecture, except that we have multiple distributional actor-critic heads. Specifically, we refer to each distributional actor-critic pair (policy + return distribution) as a head. Each episode of trajectory is rolled out by only one of the heads sampled uniformly randomly, and the collected data is trained on by all of the heads for data efficiency. The head that generated the trajectory learns on-policy, whilst all other heads learn from the same batch of data off-policy. Throughout training, the heads are updated by different gradients because they were initialized differently and learn from their own Bellman target which entails random sampling from their own return distributions at subsequent steps. This ensures a diversity in policies, giving rise to the effect of Thompson sampling.

The training of BoP entails an outer loop of three stages: a roll-out stage, a data-driven estimation stage, and an update stage. The majority of the algorithm is the same as that of BDPG, we only highlight the different or extra aspects incurred by using multiple distributional actor-critic heads, as well as the heed we paid to maintain diversity. During the roll-out stage, at the start of each episode, the agent selects a head uniformly at random, which we call the active head k, and executes actions according to the policy of that head for the duration of the whole episode. Thus, the sequence of collected transitions (s_t, a_t, r_t) is determined entirely by the policy of the active head as a behaviour policy. Meanwhile, the other heads still compute the log-probability of the selected action $\log \pi^i(a_t|s_t)$, and form an estimation of the return distribution for each state in the episode by generating a sample g_t^i from each distributional critic. These local evaluations are used to provide them with a unique sample estimate of the learning objective when updating their parameters.

During the sample estimate stage, the agent computes the advantages A_t^i and the Bellman targets x_t^i, both being unique for each respective head. These local estimates also engender a local curiosity bonus $\hat{r}_t^i$ that is proportional to the entropy reduction in the latent space conditioned on the return space. This condition is a more accurate estimate (the on-policy Bellman target x_t^k) than a model prediction (a sample from the model g_t^i):

Table 1. Hyperparameters for implementing BoP model on Atari games.

Hyperparameter	Value	Hyperparameter	Value
Num. parallel envs	16	Eval. frequency	Every 2e4 timesteps
Num. stacked frames	4	Num. heads	Variable
GAE λ	0.95	Discount γ	0.99
Num. episodes per roll-out	4	Minibatch size	256
Roll-out timesteps	128	Value loss weight	0.5
Entropy coefficient	0.01	Learning rate	Linearly 2.5e4 $\rightarrow$ 0
PPO clip range	Linearly 0.1 $\rightarrow$ 0	Curiosity	Mixed
Actor-critics updated	All, on all data	x_t^i computed by	Critic i
Actions @ roll-out	Sampled	Actions @ testing	Greedy

$$\hat{r}_t^i \propto \text{Information\_gain}(s_t, i)$$
$$:= \text{KL}\big(q_\phi(\cdot|x_t^k, s_t) \ || \ q_\phi(\cdot|g_t^i, s_t)\big), \tag{2}$$

in which the state s_t is generated by the active head k. The entropy reduction, or equivalently, information gain, quantifies the epistemic uncertainty about how well each head is modelling the return distribution. The posterior x_t^k is shared across heads as it is the only Bellman backup target among all x_t^i that is estimated on-policy and thus suffers the least degree of bias/variance. The curiosity bonus is then added to the external reward for computing the augmented advantage function that would be used to update the local policies.

During the update stage, all policies π^i are updated on the data generated by the active policy π^k. The active head is updated on-policy as in BDPG. For the other heads we use an off-policy advantage function estimated with V-trace (Espeholt et al., 2018) at each timestep. Subsequently, each head's critic is updated by minimizing a Wasserstein distance between its current return distribution model and the distribution of a Bellman target estimated from its own predictions at subsequent timesteps. Like BDPG, this is achieved by minimizing the squared distance between Bellman target x_t^i and sample g_t^i while in the meantime enforcing joint-contrastive learning adversarially.

We used a single common set of hyperparameters for implementing the BoP on Atari as shown in Table 1. The choices for the number of heads were laid out in Table 2. The policy heads are updated by Proximal Policy Optimization (PPO) (Schulman et al., 2017).

4.2   Design Considerations and Implications

In this subsection we discuss the possible variants of BoP enabled by its ensemble characteristic, and which of them are conducive to diversity. To understand these and the design decisions leading to the final settings described above, we first explain the need for diversification and the off-policy side of our framework.

Note that the following considerations for diversification are not entailed in ensemble methods applied to scalar RL, where behaviour and model diversity is much easier to uphold, i.e., a surprising backup target is considered unseen in a scalar model but merely less likely in a distribution model. Thus, the same level of diversity would provide lesser learning signal to the latter. This means if the posterior over return distributions is not sufficiently diverse, which would happen if ensemble techniques and DiRL were naively combined, the return distribution models will only tweak the likelihood for the current backup target rather than fundamentally change its return prediction; and the ensemble members remain similar after light update, forming a vicious cycle.

With multiple heads that are being maintained in BoP, each head i can form a return estimate g_t^i at the current timestep and produce a Bellman target x_t^i by sampling from itself for each of the future timesteps. Thus, there are choices about sharing these targets or not across heads in two domains: 1. to update the critic and 2. to compute the local curiosity bonus.

First we considered sharing the Bellman target x_t^k across critics, i.e., using the target of the current active head k to update all critics. We found that in practice sharing Bellman targets causes the diversity between policies to collapse, as measured by various metrics such as the sum of all absolute differences between the assigned probabilities of any two policies and the cosine similarity between two policies. This resulted in poorer exploration outcomes than with individual Bellman targets. Therefore, in the final BoP framework, the on-policy Bellman target is not shared and each critic head is trained against its own target, which provides (more) unique bootstrapped signals to each head. Formally, we use the following variation of the distributional Bellman equation:

$$\mathcal{T}^{\pi^k} G^{\pi^i}(s_t) \overset{D}{=} r_t + \gamma G^{\pi^i}(s_{t+1}) \tag{3}$$

$$s_{t+1} \sim P(s_{t+1}|s_t, a_t), \ a_t \sim \pi^k(s_t).$$

Since the states, actions and rewards are collected by the active head k, only this head is trained on-policy, while all other heads are trained off-policy. Thus, the final version of BoP is a mix of on-policy and off-policy learning, in contrast to other algorithms (Bellemare et al., 2017, Mnih et al., 2016, Li and Faisal, 2021, Osband et al., 2016, Dabney et al., 2018b), which are either one or the other.

Each distributional actor-critic member in BoP has a curiosity bonus $\hat{r}_t^i$ applied to its personal policy. We have discussed the reason for sharing the posterior return estimate x_t^k in Eq. (2) which is for its accuracy, we here consider the choices for the prior g_t. This prior can either be computed from that head itself $\mathrm{KL}\big(q(\cdot|x_t^k, s_t) \ || \ q(\cdot|g_t^i, s_t)\big)$ as in Eq. (2) or shared $\mathrm{KL}\big(q(\cdot|x_t^k, s_t) \ || \ q(\cdot|g_t^k, s_t)\big)$, where $q(z|x, s)$ is the variational encoder for the return distribution. We use local return samples g_t^i as prior to compute the information gain. This is because a surprising sample to one return distribution model might not surprise another, and each model should keep track of its accuracy to correctly bias local action selection, so that the model agreement on policies informs also implicitly the agreement on the level of surprise.

Next, we consider the schedule for updating heads: we can update all of them on every batch of freshly collected data, or just some of them. It is indeed feasible to update only one head - e.g. the active one or the most uncertain one, as measured by the curiosity bonuses. By updating only the most uncertain head at each iteration, the agent maximizes the reduction in epistemic uncertainty while still keeping the heads sufficiently diverse (by updating only one head in each update iteration). However, we found in practice that this diminishes sample efficiency due to limiting the number of heads being trained with a given amount of data. Similar empirical findings were made when training with other setups that selectively update members like updating a randomly sampled head according to its epistemic uncertainty, or training each head on 50% of their most uncertain samples. For that reason in BoP we update all heads on all the data, which provides the fastest learning at no cost of sacrificing sufficient diversity of the heads and therefore maximizes their ensemble benefits on balance.

During testing, on the other hand, the question arises as to how action selection should be performed now that we have multiple policies. BoP selects an action by averaging the action distributions of all policy heads and then chooses the greedy action from that distribution (Wiering and van Hasselt, 2008). Since all policies in our implementation are Gaussian, this is easy to realize. In practice we observed more stable performance and higher scores when using this "average-then-argmax" approach compared to other options, such as each head picking their greedy action and then performing a majority vote selection of the most popular/similar action across heads ("argmax-then-vote"), or even selecting actions only from one randomly selected head ("sample-then-argmax"). The benefits of the "average-then-argmax" tactic over the others result from relying on model agreement which is what has been truly learned and understood rather than uncertainty-quenching exploration.

Finally, we considered how to choose the number of ensemble members. We found that a small number of 3 to 5 heads strikes a good balance between effective exploration and training speed. For calibration of this statement, we found that each additional head adds about 15% more FLOPS to the total amount of computation. This increase in performance from having many heads saturates as policies start to converge and thus become more and more correlated, which justifies using a small number of heads to increase performance and exploration efficiency without excessively increasing training time.

5   Experimental Results

We tested the performance of BoP on a diverse set of Atari environments, and compared to three baselines with which BoP shares similarity in different aspects: to Bootstrapped DQN (Osband et al., 2016) as an ensemble-based exploration in scalar RL, to BDPG (Li and Faisal, 2021) as a locally optimistic DiRL exploration approach and the algorithm we build upon, and to A3C (Mnih et al., 2016) which facilitates covering extensive data space mainly by deploying multiple workers in parallel. The set of Atari environments were chosen to represent an

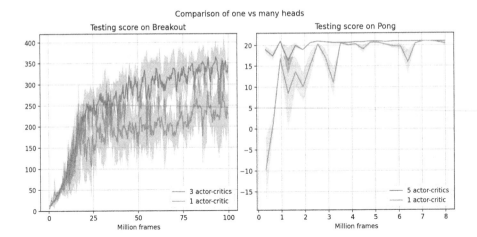

Fig. 3. Comparison of BoP with one $(K = 1)$ vs many heads $(K = 3)$ or $(K = 5)$ on Breakout and Pong. The shading shows one standard error from the mean. Exponential smoothing was applied for the scores on Breakout. The numbers of heads in multi-head cases shown are the minimal numbers that enable significant improvement over one-head baseline.

exemplar mix of hard exploration environments. Pixel-based observations were pre-processed by standard Atari wrappers as laid out in (Dabney et al. 2018b), including cropping the image frame, using only grayscaled frames, frame stacking, and taking the maximum values of any two consecutive frames.

First, we compare performances between BDPG and BoP on Freeway, Hero and MsPacman, with learning curves shown in Fig. 2. Compared to BDPG, BoP improves significantly on sample efficiency, albeit not necessarily on asymptotic performance. We note that the essential difference between BDPG and BoP is that BoP is a bootstrapped ensemble of BDPG, so the improvement of learning speed is in principle attributed to the ensemble effect. However, at this stage, it cannot be decided if it is the deep exploration enabled by Thompson sampling or the sheer multitude of workers that has resulted the advantage of ensemble technique.

To this end, we move on to investigate the impact of the number of ensemble members, i.e. heads, on a multi-worker agent's performance. In Table 2, we compare BoP against multi-worker/multi-head methods Bootrapped DQN and A3C. Although BoP does not beat baselines on all selected environments, we can see that it frequently outperforms them. Crucially, the number of heads for A3C $(K = 16)$ and Bootstrapped DQN $(K = 10)$, as proposed by their original publications, are substantially higher than those needed for BoP $(K = 3$ or in two cases $K = 5)$. Moreover, for all games where deep exploration is essential (such as MsPacman and Frostbite), BoP substantially outperforms baselines by 50%–200%. These promising results suggest that increasing the multitude of workers alone is not key to better performance. Combining with the observations made in comparing to BDPG, one can establish that the strengths of BoP are

Table 2. The testing results achieved across 3 runs. The number of heads ("#") for BoP were set by us, the ones for A3C and Bootstrapped DQN ("Boot") were set in their original works (Mnih et al., 2016, Osband et al., 2016).

Atari env	#	BoP	#	A3C	#	Boot
Freeway	3	**34**	16	0.1	10	**34**
Breakout	3	686	16	682	10	**855**
Hero	3	**37,728**	16	32,464	10	21,021
MsPacman	3	**9,057**	16	654	10	2,983
Qbert	3	**20,583**	16	15,149	10	15,092
Alien	5	**5,470**	16	518	10	2,436
Asterix	5	**42,500**	16	22,141	10	19,713
Frostbite	3	**5,940**	16	191	10	2,181
Amidar	5	1,123	16	264	10	**1,272**
BeamRider	3	6,499	16	22,708	10	**23,429**
StarGunner	3	56,200	16	**138,218**	10	55,725
Seaquest	3	2,027	16	2,355	10	**9,083**

attributed to deep exploration. In the meantime, we also observed that BoP is not as competitive in less exploration-demanding games with moving targets, such as BeamRider and Seaquest. We surmise that this is because BoP became overly explorative seeing the moving subjects whereas the motion could not be accounted for by being bold unlike in the case of Freeway.

Another experiment carried out to investigate the ensemble effect is to compare a one-head BoP against a few-head BoP (Fig. 3). We noted a substantial improvement when the number of heads increased from one to even a very small value (e.g. 3), while being a qualitative transformation from a flat algorithm into an ensemble one. This finding reinforces the notion that the benefit of BoP is not due to merely more workers, but a fundamentally distinct way that an ensemble method works in – by posterior sampling and therefore favouring uncertain areas for exploration.

This performance improvement outweighs the increase in compute time for a few-head BoP. This is probably due to the better exploration capability of each head operating with an independently updated policy learning from its own estimation errors so that an action is selected either because it is agreed to be relatively certainly optimal or is uncertain. However, when the number of ensemble members becomes too large, BoP will have lost its advantage. As mentioned earlier, we observed that on Atari each additional head adds about 15% more FLOPS for the full duration of the training compared to having only one head. This linear relationship holds true also when having 10 or 15 heads. The marginal cost in terms of FLOPS is constant. The marginal benefit from adding another head decreases with the number of heads quickly, resulting in our lower use of heads than other multi-worker algorithms. In conclusion, BoP is most advantageous when using a handful of members.

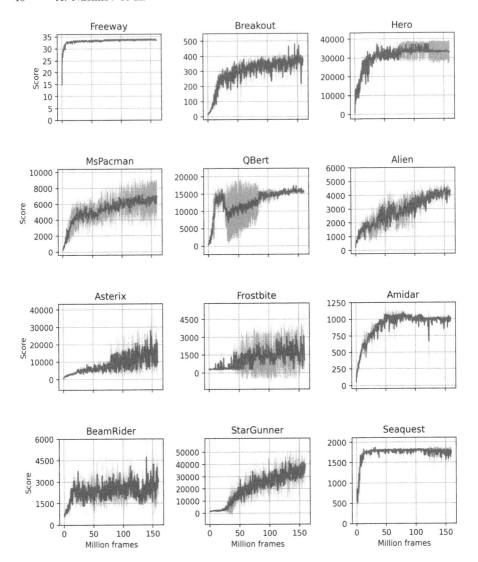

Fig. 4. Testing scores for BoP on Atari. We test the agent periodically while training. Shaded areas indicate variation in performance across multiple runs.

The learning curves of all Atari environments that BoP was tested on can be found in Fig. 4. For instance, Frostbite is a game that needs very specific sequences of actions, similar to maze games like MsPacman or QBert that require deep exploration, as decisions which one takes early on have long term impacts.

6   Discussion and Future Work

The Bag of Policies (BoP) algorithm presented here is a multi-head distributional estimator applicable to a large class of algorithms and thus extends deep exploration to distributional RL settings. Our most salient finding is that the benefits of the optimism in the face of uncertainty *can accumulate* for DiRL exploration, as we were able to substantially improve upon a DiRL approach that is optimistic on per-state basis simply by making an ensemble of it and performing Thompson sampling. This suggests that at least in DiRL, Thompson sampling and curiosity bonus, although both facilitate optimism, can work in conjunction to enhance performance further.

In addition, as our experimental results showed, the advantage of BoP is not attributed to the mere multitude of workers as BoP can surpass other multi-worker/multi-head algorithms with much fewer heads, and boost performance considerably with a few-head BoP compared to its one-head counterpart. These experiments substantiate that the ensemble technique which empowers BoP functions in a fundamentally different fashion than naively summing up the efforts of parallel workers.

On average, BoP achieves better learning speed and asymptotic performance than baselines. We have observed the biggest improvement from baselines in maze-like games like MsPacman or QBert where the agent has to choose a path in a labyrinth while collecting various items scattered throughout it and avoiding the enemies many moves down the line. These kinds of environments require deep exploration and the agent can experience vastly different outcomes depending on which path it takes. Hence, these environments provide a good example where the BoP exploration capabilities can improve the agent's performance.

In a nutshell, BoP has demonstrated that not only deep exploration is viable in DiRL, offering extensions to any DiRL settings (such as (Bellemare et al., 2017, Dabney et al., 2018a; 2018b, Freirich et al., 2019, Doan et al., 2018, Martin et al., 2020, Barth-Maron et al., 2018, Singh et al., 2020, Kuznetsov et al., 2020, Choi et al., 2019)), but also that deep exploration can further improve learning from an already optimistic exploration strategy.

Acknowledgment. We are grateful for our funding support. At the time of this work, GL and AF are sponsored by UKRI Turing AI Fellowship (EP/V025449/1), LL and FV by the PhD scholarship of the Department of Computing, Imperial College London.

References

Barth-Maron, G., et al.: Distributed distributional deterministic policy gradients. In: Proceedings of the 6th International Conference on Learning Representations (ICLR) (2018)

Bellemare, M.G., Naddaf, Y., Veness, J., Bowling, M.: The arcade learning environment: an evaluation platform for general agents. J. Artif. Intell. Res. **47**, 253–279 (2013)

Bellemare, M.G., Dabney, W., Munos, R.: A distributional perspective on reinforcement learning. In: Proceedings of the 34th International Conference on Machine Learning, vol. 70, pp. 449–458 (2017)

Chen, R.Y., Sidor, S., Abbeel, P., Schulman, J.: UCB exploration via q-ensembles (2017)

Choi, Y., Lee, K., Oh, S.: Distributional deep reinforcement learning with a mixture of Gaussians. In: 2019 International Conference on Robotics and Automation (ICRA), pp. 9791–9797 (2019)

Dabney, W., Ostrovski, G., Silver, D., Munos, R.: Implicit quantile networks for distributional reinforcement learning. In: Proceedings of the 35th International Conference on Machine Learning, vol. 80, pp. 1096–1105 (2018a)

Dabney, W., Rowland, M., Bellemare, M.G., Munos, R.: Distributional reinforcement learning with quantile regression. In: Proceedings of the AAAI Conference on Artificial Intelligence (2018b)

Doan, T., Mazoure, B., Lyle, C.: GAN q-learning (2018)

Donahue, J., Krähenbühl, P., Darrell, T.: Adversarial feature learning. In: Proceedings of the 5th International Conference on Learning Representations (ICLR) (2017)

Efron, B., Tibshirani, R.J.: An Introduction to the Bootstrap. CRC Press, Boca Raton (1994)

Espeholt, L., et al.: IMPALA: scalable distributed deep-RL with importance weighted actor-learner architectures. In: Proceedings of the 35th International Conference on Machine Learning, vol. 80, pp. 1407–1416, Stockholmsmässan, Stockholm (2018)

Freirich, D., Shimkin, T., Meir, R., Tamar, A.: Distributional multivariate policy evaluation and exploration with the bellman GAN. In: Proceedings of the 36th International Conference on Machine Learning (ICML), Long Beach, CA, USA, vol. 97, pp. 1983–1992 (2019)

Kuznetsov, A., Shvechikov, P., Grishin, A., Vetrov, D.: Controlling overestimation bias with truncated mixture of continuous distributional quantile critics. In: Proceedings of the 37th International Conference on Machine Learning (2020)

Li, L., Faisal, A.: Bayesian distributional policy gradients. In: Proceedings of the AAAI Conference on Artificial Intelligence, vol. 35, no. 1, pp. 8429–8437 (2021)

Liang, J., Makoviychuk, V., Handa, A., Chentanez, N., Macklin, M., Fox, D.: GPU-accelerated robotic simulation for distributed reinforcement learning. In: Conference on Robot Learning, pp. 270–282. PMLR (2018)

Lyle, C., Bellemare, M.G., Castro, P.S.: A comparative analysis of expected and distributional reinforcement learning. In: Proceedings of the AAAI Conference on Artificial Intelligence, vol. 33, pp. 4504–4511 (2019)

Martin, J., Lyskawinski, M., Li, X., Englot, B.: Stochastically dominant distributional reinforcement learning. In: Proceedings of the 37th International Conference on Machine Learning (2020)

Mavrin, B., et al.: Distributional reinforcement learning for efficient exploration. In: Proceedings of the 36th International Conference on Machine Learning, vol. 97, pp. 4424–4434 (2019)

Mnih, V., et al.: Asynchronous methods for deep reinforcement learning. In: Proceedings of The 33rd International Conference on Machine Learning, vol. 48, pp. 1928–1937 (2016)

O'Donoghue, B., Osband, I., Munos, R., Mnih, V.: The uncertainty Bellman equation and exploration. In: Proceedings of the 35th International Conference on Machine Learning, vol. 80, pp. 3839–3848. Stockholmsmässan, Stockholm (2018)

Osband, I., Blundell, C., Pritzel, A., Van Roy, B.: Deep exploration via Bootstrapped DQN. Adv. Neural. Inf. Process. Syst. **29**, 4026–4034 (2016)

Osband, I., Van Roy, B., Russo, D.J., Wen, Z.: Deep exploration via randomized value functions. J. Mach. Learn. Res. **20**, 1–62 (2019)

Puterman, M.L.: Markov Decision Processes: Discrete Stochastic Dynamic Programming. Wiley, Hoboken (1994)

Schulman, J., Moritz, P., Levine, S., Jordan, M., Abbeel, P.: High-dimensional continuous control using generalized advantage estimation. In: Proceedings of the 4th International Conference on Learning Representations (ICLR) (2016)

Schulman, J., Wolski, F., Dhariwal, P., Radford, A., Klimov, O.: Proximal policy optimization algorithms. arXiv preprint arXiv:1707.06347 (2017)

Singh, R., Lee, K., Chen, Y.: Sample-based distributional policy gradient (2020)

Sutton, R.S.: Policy gradient methods for reinforcement learning with function approximation. Adv. Neural. Inf. Process. Syst. **12**, 1057–1063 (1999)

Tang, Y., Agrawal, S.: Exploration by distributional reinforcement learning. In: Proceedings of the 27th International Joint Conference on Artificial Intelligence, pp. 2710–2716 (2020)

Thompson, W.R.: On the theory of apportionment. Am. J. Math. **57**(2), 450–456 (1935)

Wiering, M.A., van Hasselt, H.P.: Ensemble algorithms in reinforcement learning. IEEE Trans. Syst. Man Cybern. Part B **38**(4), 930–936 (2008)

Zhang, Z., Chen, J., Chen, Z., Li, W.: Asynchronous episodic deep deterministic policy gradient: toward continuous control in computationally complex environments. IEEE Trans. Cybern. **51**, 604–613 (2019)

Defensive Perception: Estimation and Monitoring of Neural Network Performance Under Deployment

Hendrik Vogt[1]([✉]), Stefan Buehler[1], and Mark Schutera[1,2]

[1] ZF Friedrichshafen AG, Friedrichshafen, Germany
{hendrik.vogt,stefan.buehler,mark.schutera}@zf.com
[2] Karlsruhe Institute of Technology, Karlsruhe, Germany
mark.schutera@kit.edu

Abstract. In this paper, we propose a method for addressing the issue of unnoticed catastrophic deployment and domain shift in neural networks for semantic segmentation in autonomous driving. Our approach is based on the idea that deep learning-based perception for autonomous driving is uncertain and best represented as a probability distribution. As autonomous vehicles' safety is paramount, it is crucial for perception systems to recognize when the vehicle is leaving its operational design domain, anticipate hazardous uncertainty, and reduce the performance of the perception system. To address this, we propose to encapsulate the neural network under deployment within an uncertainty estimation envelope that is based on the epistemic uncertainty estimation through the Monte Carlo Dropout approach. This approach does not require modification of the deployed neural network and guarantees expected model performance. Our *defensive perception envelope* has the capability to estimate a neural network's performance, enabling monitoring and notification of entering domains of reduced neural network performance under deployment. Furthermore, our envelope is extended by novel methods to improve the application in deployment settings, including reducing compute expenses and confining estimation noise. Finally, we demonstrate the applicability of our method for multiple different potential deployment shifts relevant to autonomous driving, such as transitions into the night, rainy, or snowy domain. Overall, our approach shows great potential for application in deployment settings and enables operational design domain recognition via uncertainty, which allows for defensive perception, safe state triggers, warning notifications, and feedback for testing or development and adaptation of the perception stack.

Keywords: Autonomous Driving · Safety Envelope · Computer Vision · Monte Carlo Dropout · Epistemic Uncertainty

1 Introduction

The ability to accurately perceive semantic information is critical in autonomous driving and automotive vision. Neural networks can perform this task through

F. Cuzzolin and M. Sultana (Eds.): Epi UAI 2023, LNAI 14523, pp. 44–58, 2024.
https://doi.org/10.1007/978-3-031-57963-9_4

semantic segmentation, where a neural network assigns a class label to each pixel of an input image (Xue et al., 2018). State-of-the-art semantic segmentation models have achieved high performance across a wide range of scenarios and domains (Behley et al., 2019, Yu et al., 2020).

Pixel-wise semantic segmentation is the task of assigning every pixel of the input image a class prediction. Because every pixel is classified with a value, semantic segmentation is capable of drawing fine outlines, generating high-semantic information central to modern perception within autonomous driving. In this work, we utilize DeeplabV3+ (Chen et al., 2018) as a base model for pixel-wise semantic segmentation and modify it for use with Monte Carlo Dropout. By inserting dropout layers (Gal and Ghahramani, 2016) after every 2D convolution layer, we demonstrate that any model can be modified to perform Monte Carlo Dropout, even after training.

Deploying neural networks as part of the perception system for an autonomous vehicle requires a clear understanding of the operational design domain (ODD) in which the vehicle will operate. Therefore, the ODD is defined explicitly, and data is gathered and used to optimize and validate the neural network for this specific domain. However, in real-world applications, deep convolutional neural networks (CNNs) may be exposed to substantially different data from the training data, leading to a phenomenon known as deployment shift (Chan et al., 2021, Schutera et al., 2019). This deployment shift can occur due to various reasons like a change in time of day, weather, landmarks, object appearance, and traffic conditions, making it impossible to consider every possible scenario, use case, and road condition while defining the ODD (Berman, 2019). The limitations of ODD definitions in ensuring safety in autonomous driving are highlighted by the effect that it cannot cover every possibility of change in the real world, which may cause severe security risk and fatalities (Banks et al., 2018, Hüllermeier and Waegeman, 2021, National Highway Traffic Safety Administration, 2022). Hence, there is an emerging need for autonomous systems to recognize and understand when they are in unknown and potentially unsafe situations, especially during inference when the system has been deployed. Safety-inducing strategies that detect unknown situations and transition the system into a safe state referred to as defensive perception are required. The perception system needs to have a mechanism to detect when it is leaving the ODD and anticipate hazardous uncertainty, which reduces the performance of the perception system.

As previously stated, deployment shift, the phenomenon of a neural network being exposed to data from a different domain than its training data, can occur in real-world applications of autonomous vehicles. However, detecting deployment shift is difficult due to the lack of correlation between deployment shift and drop in prediction confidence, as highlighted by Nguyen et al. in (Nguyen et al., 2015).

Several state-of-the-art approaches have been proposed to address this issue of out-of-domain detection and uncertainty estimation in deep neural networks as discussed in (Gawlikowski et al., 2021). For instance, Du et al. proposed Virtual Outlier Synthesis (VOS) (Du et al., 2022), a method that synthesizes outliers for additional training to generate a clear boundary between in- and out-of-domain data. Another approach (Chan et al., 2021) shows that by retraining a semantic segmentation model on unknown objects to maximize the prediction's softmax entropy, the uncertainty of specific out-of-domain object instances can be detected. Additionally, deploying auxiliary models such as an Essence Neural Network (Blazek and Lin, 2021), a Posterior Neural Network (Charpentier et al., 2020), or Meta Classifiers (Rottmann et al., 2018) enables the estimation of domain affiliation or uncertainty of a sample's prediction.

While these approaches may require additional models, architectural adaptions (Sensoy et al., 2018) or dedicated training processes (Van Amersfoort et al., 2020), another alternative is to use minimally invasive approaches such as Monte Carlo Dropout (Rottmann and Schubert, 2019) for estimating epistemic uncertainty in deep neural networks.

Conventional neural networks struggle to express prediction confidence, especially when leaving the source domain they have been trained on.

As dropout at first was introduced to prevent a neural network from overfitting and thus was only applied at training to generalize the model's prediction (Hinton et al., 2012) especially Monte Carlo Dropout later was introduced as a method to measure the model's uncertainty of non-Bayesian neural networks by applying the Monte Carlo Dropout also during inference and determine its predictive distribution (Gal and Ghahramani, 2016).

Monte Carlo Dropout mimics multiple sub-network prediction distributions $q(\mathbf{y}|\mathbf{x})$ by deploying dropout layers throughout the complete network and multiple forward passes T. While W_i denotes the networks weight matrices and L enumerates the model's layer. The deviations in the sub-networks' predictions $\hat{\mathbf{y}}$ are then utilized to express the epistemic uncertainty of the entire model on a single frame $\mathbf{x}$ - referred to as Monte Carlo Dropout, giving the estimated approximate predictive distribution:

$$\mathbb{E}_{q(\mathbf{y}|\mathbf{x})}(\mathbf{y}) \approx \frac{1}{T} \sum_{t=1}^{T} \hat{\mathbf{y}}(\mathbf{x}, \mathbf{W}_1^t, \ldots, \mathbf{W}_L^t). \tag{1}$$

In this paper, we propose a method for estimating epistemic uncertainty during the inference of semantic neural networks for autonomous driving using Monte Carlo Dropout, as the widely accepted uncertainty measurement at inference (Labach et al., 2019). In contrast to the other state of the art uncertainty measurements mentioned above using other techniques than the Monte Carlo Dropout, the here presented approach aims to be applicable on any neural network at inference and in real time without making changes at training and or test time as well as it does not require additional data.

Incorporation into our *defensive perception envelope*, which monitors uncertainty during deployment, demonstrates that epistemic uncertainty can serve as a proxy for model performance. This novel approach allows us to detect when the system is operating outside of its intended domain and provides an online cue for prediction performance. Furthermore, by imposing thresholds on the uncertainty value, we can define triggers that can be used to implement safety measures such as warning notifications for the driver or even transitions into a *safe state* where the vehicle engages other safety systems and for example, reduces its speed. The main contributions of this paper are:

- A safety envelope that integrates Monte Carlo Dropout (Labach et al., 2019) into semantic segmentation for autonomous driving scenarios.
- A novel entropy measure that captures model performance and domain shifts during deployment and inference.
- An adaptation of the Monte Carlo Dropout method that utilizes rolling forward passes to improve computational efficiency during deployment.

2   Novel Methods and Metrics

2.1   Novel Concept for Defensive Perception

In the following, we present a detailed overview of our proposed method for estimating uncertainty and monitoring the performance of neural networks during deployment. Our approach utilizes a *defensive perception envelope*, which is wrapped around a given perception algorithm. Typically, the performance of a neural network is evaluated by comparing its predictions to manually labeled data (ground truth). However, such labeled data is unavailable during online inference in autonomous driving. To address this, our *defensive perception envelope* indirectly estimates the neural network's performance using Monte Carlo Dropout, enabling real-time performance estimation during deployment. Figure 1 illustrates the schematic of our proposed framework.

Training and Validation. The base of our approach is a perception neural network θ_S that solves a task such as pixel-wise semantic segmentation. The neural network is therefore trained, validated, and released for deployment in the source domain S with samples $\mathbf{x}_S$ from the said domain.

Model Deployment. For deployment, the model is modified by inserting dropout layers (Gal and Ghahramani, 2016) after every 2D convolution layer. The modification prepares the neural network for the Monte Carlo Dropout approach of our *defensive perception envelope.*

Data with Deployment Shift. During deployment, due to a domain shift, the neural network is prone to encounter samples $\mathbf{x}_{S+1}$, which are outside of the source domain. There are numerous reasons for a domain shift, including deployment shifts and other ODD shifts that have not been considered during training and validation. The emerging shifts and the resulting potential drop in performance are critical as they occur silently and result in unnoticed catastrophic deployment.

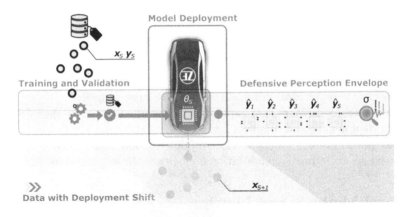

Neural Network Performance Estimation and Monitoring under Deployment

Fig. 1. System Flow Overview - within an autonomous driving platform supported by a perception stack, the perception model θ_S is trained and validated for a given source domain S. Deployed in the vehicle the *defensive perception envelope* generates five outputs $\mathcal{Y} = \{\hat{\mathbf{y}}_1, \ldots, \hat{\mathbf{y}}_5\}$ with Monte Carlo Dropout. Suppose a sample with a domain shift $\mathbf{x}_{S+1}$ is fed to the perception model θ_S, the uncertainty of the output vectors for this sample rises, and the *defensive perception envelope* informs the system that it enters a domain with high uncertainty. These notifications are triggered by a pre-selected threshold σ.

Defensive Perception Envelope. Monte Carlo Dropout determines the uncertainty u_t for a sample $\mathbf{x}_t$ at time t. The uncertainty is calculated by multiple forward passes n of the same sample while randomly dropping different weights. The fluctuation in the predictions $\hat{\mathbf{y}}_t \in \{\hat{\mathbf{y}}_{t,1}, \ldots, \hat{\mathbf{y}}_{t,n}\}$ is mapped to an uncertainty metric (see Subsect. 2.2). The *defensive perception envelope* is configured permissive or stringent by introducing uncertainty thresholds based on the system characteristics. The uncertainty threshold can be based on the uncertainty value distribution computed on the overall data. Further, multiple thresholds enable triggers for multiple stages of defensive reactions, such as system notification, vehicle slow-down, and the safe-state transition.

2.2 Pseudo Cross-Entropy for Uncertainty During Inference

At the core of our uncertainty metric resides the cross-entropy CE metric. As input, the cross-entropy expects a probability distribution $\mathbf{q}$ of the prediction vector $\hat{\mathbf{y}}$, in the form of a normalized exponential function over all predictable classes $c \in \mathbf{C}$, such as given by a softmax layer,

$$\mathbf{q}_c = \frac{e^{\hat{\mathbf{y}}_c}}{\sum_i^{\mathbf{C}} e^{\hat{\mathbf{y}}_i}}. \tag{2}$$

The entropy $\mathbf{H}$ of a prediction vector $\mathbf{q}$ is calculated by multiplication with the true distribution $\mathbf{p}$. During deployment, a true distribution is not given; thus, the approach makes use of a pseudo ground truth approximation $\mathbf{p}_i \approx \tilde{\mathbf{y}}'_i$,

$$H(\mathbf{p}, \mathbf{q}) = - \sum_i^{\mathbf{C}} \tilde{\mathbf{y}}'_i \, log(\mathbf{q}_i). \tag{3}$$

Assuming that a true prediction is linked with a single class, the pseudo ground truth is approximated as a one-hot-encoding of the prediction vector $\mathbf{q}$, resulting in the pseudo cross-entropy CE',

$$CE' = -log(\frac{e^{\hat{y}_c}}{\sum_i^{\mathbf{C}} e^{\hat{y}_i}}). \tag{4}$$

In order to deploy the pseudo cross-entropy as an uncertainty measure of a neural network's prediction, further requirements need to be fulfilled:

– The pseudo cross-entropy needs to depict the entropy emerging from multiple forward passes T.
– The entropy needs to be independent of the number of forward passes n.
– Entropy should follow an exponential function to smooth uncertainty for small deviations while upscaling larger deviations.
– For comparability, the range of values needs to be confined to $CE' \in [0, 1]$.

To measure the uncertainty over multiple forward passes, the one-hot encoded output vector $\mathbf{y}_{fwp}$ from each forward pass (fwp) is taken, and the hits for each class are accumulated. The retrieved vector $\mathbf{v}_{hC}$ shows the distribution of hits over all classes for the number of applied forward passes. As only the classes, which are predicted in at least one of the forward passes, are of interest, any class with 0 hits is removed from this vector so that $\mathbf{v}_{hC} \setminus \{0\}$, and respective a class i is represented by $\mathcal{C}_h$.

From this vector, the class with the maximum number of hits is assumed to be the true class, hence a pseudo ground truth $max(\mathbf{v}_{hC})$ (equal to $\mathbf{p}$ in Eq. 3) is determined. In the case of two or more classes having the maximum number of hits, the class with the lowest index is taken as the pseudo ground truth, following the implementation of the used $argmax$ function, provided by the python library NumPy (Harris et al., 2020).

The here presented formula fulfilling the requirements mentioned above is:

$$CE_u = 1 - \frac{\exp(\frac{max(\mathbf{v}_{hC})}{n_{fwp}})}{\sum_i^{\mathcal{C}_h} \exp(\frac{\mathbf{v}_{hC}(i)}{n_{fwp}})}. \tag{5}$$

For intuitive readability, the uncertainty measurement is subtracted from one to have a low score near zero when the uncertainty of the neural network is low and a value near one when the uncertainty is critical. For semantic segmentation, the classification is done pixel-wise; hence the uncertainty is calculated on every pixel of the given input frame. In order to obtain the frame's overall uncertainty, the mean of all pixel's uncertainties is determined.

2.3   Rolling Monte Carlo Dropout

The frame rate of advanced driver assistance systems (ADAS) or autonomous vehicle perception systems must be high enough to allow the system to react on time to its surrounding environment. As a result, consecutive frames in a sequence S tend to be similar (see Subsect. 3.3). In order to reduce computational effort and increase the efficiency of the implemented *safety envelope*, we introduce the Rolling Monte Carlo Dropout method.

This method is based on the idea of a sliding window over the sequence S. Instead of applying Monte Carlo Dropout on a single image multiple times (shown in Fig. 1), the Monte Carlo Dropout is applied to a sequence of consecutive images. Sequential data allows the calculation of the modified categorical cross entropy u_t for the Rolling Monte Carlo Dropout by replacing the number of forward passes n_{fwp} with the number of images n_{img} within the stride of the defined sliding window.

$$S_t = \{\mathbf{x}_{t-n} \ldots, \mathbf{x}_t\} \tag{6}$$

$$u_t = \sum_{\mathbf{x} \in S_t} CE_u(\mathbf{x}) \tag{7}$$

The uncertainty of our measurement increases when applying the Rolling Monte Carlo Dropout method to a sequence of consecutive images rather than a single image due to the induced aleatoric uncertainty. Hence, the Rolling Monte Carlo Dropout method cannot be applied to an arbitrary number of consecutive images. Instead, the number n of images in a sequence or window is constrained by the speed range of the ego vehicle and the sensor's sampling rate, influencing the magnitude of the aleatoric uncertainty. Overall, using the Rolling Monte Carlo Dropout improves the efficiency of the *defensive perception envelope* by reducing the required number of forward passes while maintaining the model's accuracy. The operational capabilities and boundaries are the subject of study in the following experiments (see Sect. 3).

3   Experiments

In this study, we conduct experiments using two datasets: the MNIST dataset and the BDD10K dataset. The MNIST dataset, representing a simple machine learning task, is used to provide a general proof of concept for the proposed metric. The BDD10K dataset, represents a more complex task - semantic segmentation - and serves as a real-world example in the context of autonomous driving.

MNIST (LeCun et al., 2010) consists of 70,000 handwritten numbers containing the digits zero through nine and accordingly labeled, suitable for a classification task. MNIST is deployed as a toy problem, being well-known, easy to interpret, and comprehensible.

BDD10K (Yu et al., 2020) contains 9.000 images labeled pixel-wise for semantic segmentation. The images are mostly non-sequential and suitable for single-frame prediction only. The dataset is chosen for its diversity, including images from different times of day, weather conditions, and scenarios. This allows for domain shift experiments. Further, there are unlabeled video sequences that can be used for deployment and runtime experiments.

The models for each experiment are only trained on a defined source domain: for the MNIST dataset, this is non-rotated numbers, and for the BDD10K dataset, it is images recorded during the day or labeled as clear. Any data that is not part of the source domain is framed and subsequently interpreted as a domain shift. This data is then only used at inference time for validation and test purposes.

The experiments, particularly those related to semantic segmentation, are designed to demonstrate the validity of the proposed metrics and the methods underlying the *defensive perception envelope* (see Fig. 1). To apply the proposed approach, the neural network must be trained on explicit classes and should not contain any general unknown or misc class, as proposed in (Zhang and LeCun, 2017). The base dataset for these experiments is the BDD10K dataset, and the task is semantic segmentation. Training is conducted on NVIDIA P100 GPUs with Intel Xeon E5-2667 v4 CPUs. For details on neural network architecture, implementation, and tooling, see our repository[1], including a jupyter notebook kick-start demo.

3.1   How Confident Should We be About Confidence?

In the first experiment, we introduce a domain shift to the MNIST dataset by anticlockwise rotating the given samples in five-degree increments up to a total of 90°. The classifier, which is only trained on the source domain (non-rotated samples), is equipped with dropout layers. The uncertainty (as defined in Subsect. 2.2) of each domain is calculated using Monte Carlo Dropout on 20 forward passes for each sample. Since the labels and correct class for the out-of-domain samples are available, we compare the uncertainty and performance estimation to the prediction error and model confidence derived from the maximum one-hot encoded output vector of the model's prediction.

Both the error and uncertainty increase with the rotation (see Fig. 2). It is worth noting that even though the model's performance on the out-of-domain data drops by over 90%, its confidence merely drops by 14%.

This behavior is substantiated by Spearman's rank correlation coefficients (Spearman, 1904). While the uncertainty and the model error have a correlation coefficient of 0.93, the correlation coefficient of the maximum one hot encoded values with respect to the error is nine percentage points lower.

This supports the findings of Nguyen et al. (Nguyen et al., 2015), stating that a model's confidence does not reliably detect out-of-domain data. On the contrary, our proposed uncertainty metric provides a reliable performance estima-

---

[1] Defensive Perception Repository (ours): https://osf.io/fjxw3/.

tion that reflects the model's uncertainty, as evidenced by its strong correlation with the model's error. This is an important finding, as in real-world deployment scenarios, labels are typically not provided during inference, making it difficult to determine a model's performance by means of conventional offline validation.

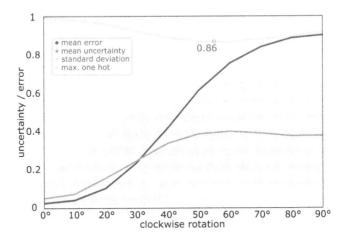

Fig. 2. This graph shows the uncertainty on the MNIST test data anticlockwise rotated up to 90°, computed with 20 forward passes and a dropout rate of 0.4. The model was trained on the MNIST (LeCun et al., 2010) training data set without any applied rotation.

3.2 Uncertainty is Able to Depict Out-of-Domain Performance

Our second experiment demonstrates the effectiveness of our proposed performance estimation method in the challenging task of semantic segmentation, where real domain shifts present in the BDD10K dataset are deployed. Specifically, we use the domain shifts from day to night, day to dawn, and clear to rainy or clear to snowy.

To evaluate the performance of our model, we train it solely on the respective source domains (day or clear) and add dropout layers during inference to enable the use of the Monte Carlo Dropout method for our proposed performance estimation. After training, the uncertainty for every sample of the source domain and the shifted domain using the Monte Carlo Dropout with a dropout rate of 0.2 and five forward passes per sample is calculated. The uncertainty is calculated for each pixel.

It can be depicted with a heat map (see Fig. 3) as done here for two randomly selected images, one from the source domain day and the other from the shifted domain night.

On both heat maps (day and night), high uncertainty is present along the edges of the segmented objects and areas. Further, in the night domain areas

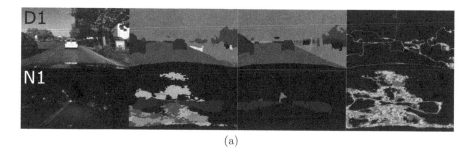

(a)

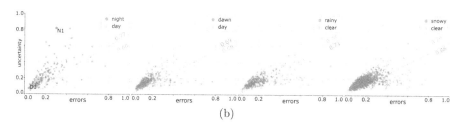

(b)

Fig. 3. Figure (a) displays randomly selected images of the BDD10K dataset from the day and night domain. Additionally, the resulting prediction of the model, the corresponding ground truth labels, and the heat map of the uncertainty values are depicted. In (b), the correlations between the model error and the computed uncertainty for the following domains are presented: day (source) - night (out-of-domain), day (source) - dawn (out-of-domain), clear (source) - rainy (out-of-domain) and clear (source) - snowy (out-of-domain). In each experiment, the model was trained solely on the respective source domain (day or clear). The uncertainty was calculated using five forward passes and a dropout rate of 0.2. For improved visibility in the plots, the uncertainty values are scaled as follows, the mean error is divided by the mean uncertainty value based on the source domain data, and the ratio is applied as a factor to each uncertainty value.

that experience information loss due to the night domain's characteristics, this is visible in large parts of the sky and the poorly illuminated driveable space. Differing pixel class predictions cause uncertainty increases during multiple forward passes - this provides an example of how a *defensive perception envelope* detects the night sample as out-of-domain (see the proposed system flow overview visualized in Fig. 1). Based on the quantification of the derived uncertainty value, the system can enact a safety countermeasure.

As the ground truth label for each sample of the source domain and the shifted domain is available, it is possible to calculate the true model error for each sample. Spearman's rank correlation coefficient (Spearman, 1904) is calculated over all samples of the source and out-of-domain data to examine the relation between the true model error and our proposed performance estimation. The validation reveals a strong correlation between the model's error and the performance estimation. For the day domain, the correlation coefficient is 0.68, while for the clear domain, it is 0.74. These source domain correlation coefficients can further serve as a reverence for the out-of-domain correlations.

Thereupon, for the out-of-domain data, strong correlations are confirmed: A correlation coefficient for the night domain of 0.77 and 0.68 for the dawn domain, as well as 0.71 for the rainy domain and 0.66 for the snowy domain, shows that the here proposed performance estimation reflects the model's error.

It is to be highlighted that the here presented technique tends to underestimate the prediction error due to a correlation coefficient below one between the model's error and the uncertainty across all examined domains.

This finding is significant for systems under deployment, as this shows that the novel approach can provide a proxy for model performance without the need for ground truth labels at runtime. Furthermore, our proposed uncertainty estimation method reliably approximates the model's prediction error, particularly on out-of-domain data (as evident in Fig. 3).

3.3   Sequential Data Allows for Compute Efficient Uncertainty Estimation

As employed in the experiments above, the vanilla Monte Carlo dropout method can become computationally expensive as it requires multiple forward passes per frame to determine the model's uncertainty on a given sample (see Fig. 1). Under deployment, perception systems are heavily limited by runtime requirements, facing limited computational resources (Hafner et al., 2022).

To address this issue, we propose a compute-efficient solution by taking advantage of the sequential nature of the input data - as it is known from a camera stream within autonomous vehicles. Furthermore, assuming that the frame rate of the input data is high enough, the differences between subsequent frames can be neglected. Thus, to obtain a sample's uncertainty and performance estimation, instead of multiple forward passes on each frame, we process subsequent frames by applying rolling forward passes (see Rolling Monte Carlo Dropout in Subsect. 2.3).

The model is again trained on the BDD10K training data set, and the experiments are executed on the 20 provided video sequences of the BDD10K. These video sequences are recorded at different locations with various driving velocities. At the same time, the frame rate is constant at 30 frames per second for each video sequence. In addition to verifying the assumption of the similarity

Table 1. The table presents the model's error based on the applied dropout rate, rounded to two significant decimals. When no dropout is applied - the dropout rate is 0 - the model's error is 0.21. This error serves as benchmark for comparing the impact of different dropout rates on the model's performance.

dropout rate	0	0.1	0.2	0.3	0.4	0.5	0.6	0.7	0.8	0.9
error	0.21	0.21	0.21	0.21	0.21	0.22	0.22	0.23	0.25	0.34

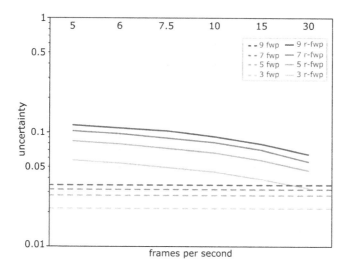

Fig. 4. This graph compares the influence of the frame rates on the uncertainty. As a baseline (dotted lines), the frame rate independent Monte Carlo Dropout with a different number of forward passes (fwp) is considered; thus, the uncertainty is calculated on only one image. The Rolling Monte Carlo Dropout (solid lines) applies rolling forward passes (r-fwp) and calculates the uncertainty on subsequent frames, which leads to a frame rate dependency. The model for this graph was trained on the BDD10k training set, and the uncertainty was calculated on the provided 20 video sequences from the BDD10k dataset. A fixed dropout rate of 0.2 is used.

of subsequent frames, it is further evaluated how the frame rate and stride of rolling forward passes affect the model's uncertainty. The stride with this defines the number of images that are considered to calculate the uncertainty and correspond to the number of forward passes in the vanilla Monte Carlo Dropout.

For 30 frames per second, the highest possible in our experiment, the uncertainty with three forward passes of the vanilla Monte Carlo Dropout is 0.022. In contrast, for three rolling forward passes, the uncertainty at 30 frames per second is 0.033 - a minor deviation of 0.011 in the uncertainty value (see Fig. 4). The slight increase in the uncertainty needs an educated trade-off against the advantage of square savings $O(n^2) \rightarrow O(n)$ in computing efforts. Accordingly, for the vanilla Monte Carlo dropout, three forward passes must be applied on each of the three consecutive frames, so nine forward passes in total. In contrast, for the Rolling Monte Carlo Dropout, only three forward passes are necessary to cover the three considered frames.

Furthermore, it is shown that the uncertainty is more sensitive to the stride of the Rolling Monte Carlo Dropout than to the number of forward passes of the vanilla Monte Carlo Dropout. For a larger number of forward passes, the uncertainty slightly increases from 0.032 (three forward passes) to 0.035 (nine forward passes). For an increasing stride, the uncertainty increases from 0.033 (stride of three frames) to 0.065 (stride of nine frames) and thus almost doubles.

The frame rate only influences the Rolling Monte Carlo Dropout. The frame rate does not affect the vanilla Monte Carlo Dropout, as its uncertainty calculation is based on a single frame. The uncertainty curvature for Rolling Monte Carlo Dropout is characteristically decreasing: The lower the frame rate, the higher the uncertainty as the difference between consecutive frames increases. For a stride of three, the uncertainty increases from 0.032 up to 0.058, and for a stride of nine, from an uncertainty of 0.065 to an uncertainty of 0.118.

In conclusion, our results indicate that by applying Rolling Monte Carlo Dropout on consecutive data with a high frame rate, square the computational effort is reduced. This finding is of major importance as computational effort is a very limited resource in autonomous driving systems. Therefore, the following section investigates the effect of the dropout rate on the inference performance.

3.4   There is No Need for a Pure Inference Pass

Dropout layers are essential for applying the (Rolling) Monte Carlo Dropout to estimate a model's uncertainty during deployment. Using the novel Rolling Monte Carlo Dropout approach, reducing the number of necessary forward passes to only one per frame is possible. As is, another forward pass without dropout is still needed to yield the semantic segmentation output of the perception stack. However, in case the dropout does not reduce the quality of the semantic segmentation during inference, the output of the forward pass with Monte Carlo Dropout can directly be used as the output of the perception stack, which would further half the remaining computational efforts.

In order to determine whether dropout affects the model's prediction performance, a model is trained on the day domain of the BDD10K training dataset. Subsequently, the model is validated on the validation data set by comparing different dropout rates against the induced error, see Table 1.

The results show that up to a dropout rate of 0.4, the error induced by dropout is smaller than 1%. For a dropout rate of up to 0.6, the error is still around 1%. However, the error rises to 0.34 for a dropout rate of 0.9. For the here presented data set, the dropout rate within a range of 0.1 to 0.6 can be safely used while maintaining the functionality of the semantic segmentation and, at the same time, reducing the computational effort within the *defensive perception envelope*.

4   Conclusion

In this paper, we proposed a method for addressing the issue of unnoticed catastrophic deployment and domain shift in neural networks for semantic segmentation in autonomous driving. Our approach is based on the idea that deep learning-based perception for autonomous driving is uncertain and best represented as a probability distribution. Furthermore, we demonstrated the applicability of our method for multiple different potential deployment shifts relevant to autonomous driving, such as entering for the model unknown domains such as night, dawn, rainy, or snowy.

Our *defensive perception envelope* encapsulates the neural network under deployment within an envelope based on the epistemic uncertainty estimation through the Monte Carlo Dropout approach. This approach does not require modification of the deployed neural network and has been shown to guarantee expected model performance. In addition, it estimates a neural network's performance, enabling monitoring and notification of entering domains of reduced neural network performance under deployment.

Furthermore, our envelope is extended by novel methods to improve the application in deployment settings, such as Rolling Monte Carlo Dropout, including reducing compute expenses and confining estimation noise. Finally, by enabling operational design domain recognition via uncertainty, our approach potentially allows for customized defensive perception, safe-state triggers, warning notifications, and feedback for testing or development of the perception stack.

The safety of autonomous vehicles is of paramount importance, and the ability to detect and respond to domain shifts is critical. Our approach shows great potential for application in deployment settings and has the capability to improve the overall safety and performance of autonomous driving systems. By making the source code publicly available, we hope to spark further research in this direction.

Acknowledgement. We want to thank our fellow researchers at Karlsruhe Institute of Technology and our colleagues at ZF Friedrichshafen AG - in particular, Dr. Jochen Abhau, and apl. Prof. Dr. Markus Reischl.

References

Banks, V.A., Plant, K.L., Stanton, N.A.: Driver error or designer error: using the perceptual cycle model to explore the circumstances surrounding the fatal tesla crash on 7th May 2016. Saf. Sci. **108**, 278–285 (2018)

Behley, J., et al.: SemanticKITTI: a dataset for semantic scene understanding of LiDAR sequences. In: Proceedings of the IEEE/CVF International Conference on Computer Vision (ICCV) (2019)

Berman, B.: The key to autonomous vehicle safety is odd (2019). https://www.sae.org/news/2019/11/odds-for-av-testing

Blazek, P.J., Lin, M.M.: Explainable neural networks that simulate reasoning. Nat. Comput. Sci. **1**(9), 607–618 (2021)

Chan, R., Rottmann, M., Gottschalk, H.: Entropy maximization and meta classification for out-of-distribution detection in semantic segmentation. In: Proceedings of the IEEE/CVF International Conference on Computer Vision, pp. 5128–5137 (2021)

Charpentier, B., Zügner, D., Günnemann, S.: Posterior network: uncertainty estimation without OOD samples via density-based pseudo-counts. Adv. Neural. Inf. Process. Syst. **33**, 1356–1367 (2020)

Chen, L.-C., Zhu, Y., Papandreou, G., Schroff, F., Adam, H.: Encoder-decoder with atrous separable convolution for semantic image segmentation. CoRR, abs/1802.02611 (2018). http://arxiv.org/abs/1802.02611

Du, X., Wang, Z., Cai, M., Li, Y.: VOS: learning what you don't know by virtual outlier synthesis. arXiv preprint arXiv:2202.01197 (2022)

Gal, Y., Ghahramani, Z.: Dropout as a bayesian approximation: appendix (2016)

Gawlikowski, J., et al.: A survey of uncertainty in deep neural networks. arXiv preprint arXiv:2107.03342 (2021)

Hafner, F.M., Zeller, M., Schutera, M., Abhau, J., Kooij, J.F.P.: Backboneanalysis: structured insights into compute platforms from CNN inference latency. In: 2022 IEEE Intelligent Vehicles Symposium (IV), pp. 1801–1809 (2022). https://doi.org/10.1109/IV51971.2022.9827260

Harris, C.R., et al.: Array programming with NumPy. Nature 585(7825), 357–362 (2020). https://doi.org/10.1038/s41586-020-2649-2

Hinton, G.E., Srivastava, N., Krizhevsky, A., Sutskever, I., Salakhutdinov, R.: Improving neural networks by preventing co-adaptation of feature detectors. CoRR, abs/1207.0580 (2012). http://arxiv.org/abs/1207.0580

Hüllermeier, E., Waegeman, W.: Aleatoric and epistemic uncertainty in machine learning: an introduction to concepts and methods. Mach. Learn. 110(3), 457–506 (2021)

Labach, A., Salehinejad, H., Valaee, S.: Survey of dropout methods for deep neural networks. arXiv e-prints, art. arXiv:1904.13310 (2019). https://doi.org/10.48550/arXiv.1904.13310

LeCun, Y., Cortes, C., Burges, C.J.C.: MNIST handwritten digit database. ATT Labs (2010). http://yann.lecun.com/exdb/mnist

National Highway Traffic Safety Administration. Summary report: Standing general order on crash reporting for automated driving systems (2022)

Nguyen, A., Yosinski, J., Clune, J.: Deep neural networks are easily fooled: high confidence predictions for unrecognizable images. In: Proceedings of the IEEE Conference on Computer Vision and Pattern Recognition, pp. 427–436 (2015)

Rottmann, M., Schubert, M.: Uncertainty measures and prediction quality rating for the semantic segmentation of nested multi resolution street scene images. In: Proceedings of the IEEE/CVF Conference on Computer Vision and Pattern Recognition Workshops, pp. 1361–1369 (2019)

Rottmann, M., Colling, P., Hack, T.-P., Hüger, F., Schlicht, P., Gottschalk, H.: Prediction error meta classification in semantic segmentation: detection via aggregated dispersion measures of softmax probabilities. CoRR abs/1811.00648 (2018)

Schutera, M., Hafner, F.M., Vogt, H., et al.: Domain is of the essence: data deployment for city-scale multi-camera vehicle re-identification. In: IEEE International Conference on Advanced Video and Signal Based Surveillance, pp. 1–6 (2019). https://doi.org/10.1109/AVSS.2019.8909858. ISSN 2643-6205

Sensoy, M., Kandemir, M., Kaplan, L.M.: Evidential deep learning to quantify classification uncertainty. CoRR, abs/1806.01768 (2018). http://arxiv.org/abs/1806.01768

Spearman, C.: The proof and measurement of association between two things. Am. J. Psychol. 15(1), 72–101 (1904). http://www.jstor.org/stable/1412159. ISSN 00029556

Van Amersfoort, J., Smith, L., Teh, Y.W., Gal, Y.: Uncertainty estimation using a single deep deterministic neural network. In: Proceedings of Machine Learning Research, vol. 119, pp. 9690–9700 (2020). https://proceedings.mlr.press/v119/van-amersfoort20a.html

Xue, J.-R., Fang, J.-W., Zhang, P.: A survey of scene understanding by event reasoning in autonomous driving. Int. J. Autom. Comput. 15(3), 249–266 (2018)

Yu, F., et al.: BDD100K: a diverse driving dataset for heterogeneous multitask learning. In: IEEE/CVF Conference on Computer Vision and Pattern Recognition (CVPR) (2020)

Zhang, X., LeCun, Y.: Universum prescription: regularization using unlabeled data. In: Proceedings of the AAAI Conference on Artificial Intelligence, vol. 31 (2017)

Towards Understanding the Interplay of Generative Artificial Intelligence and the Internet

Gonzalo Martínez[1]([envelope]) [ID], Lauren Watson[2] [ID], Pedro Reviriego[3] [ID],
José Alberto Hernández[1] [ID], Marc Juarez[2] [ID], and Rik Sarkar[2] [ID]

[1] Universidad Carlos III de Madrid, Madrid, Spain
`gonzmart@pa.uc3m.es`, `jahgutie@it.uc3m.es`
[2] School of Informatics, University of Edinburgh, Edinburgh, UK
`{lauren.watson,marc.juarez,rik.sarkar}@ed.ac.uk`
[3] Universidad Politécnica de Madrid, Madrid, Spain
`pedro.reviriego@upm.es`

Abstract. The rapid adoption of generative Artificial Intelligence (AI) tools that can generate realistic images or text, such as DALL-E, Mid-Journey, or ChatGPT, have put the societal impacts of these technologies at the center of public debate. These tools are possible due to the massive amount of data (text and images) that is publicly available through the Internet. At the same time, these generative AI tools become content creators that are already contributing to the data that is available to train future models. Therefore, future versions of generative AI tools will be trained with a mix of human-created and AI-generated content, causing a potential feedback loop between generative AI and public data repositories. This interaction raises many questions: how will future versions of generative AI tools behave when trained on a mixture of real and AI-generated data? Will they evolve and improve with the new data sets or on the contrary will they degrade? Will evolution introduce biases or reduce diversity in subsequent generations of generative AI tools? What are the societal implications of the possible degradation of these models? Can we mitigate the effects of this feedback loop? In this work, we explore the effect of this interaction and report some initial results using simple diffusion models trained with various image datasets. Our results show that the quality and diversity of the generated images can degrade over time suggesting that incorporating AI-created data can have undesired effects on future versions of generative models.

Keywords: Generative AI · Internet · Degeneration

1 Introduction

Generative AI tools like DALL-E for generating images from text descriptions or ChatGPT for generating conversation-like answers to text queries, have had a record-breaking adoption, gaining millions of users in a span of a few months. In

F. Cuzzolin and M. Sultana (Eds.): Epi UAI 2023, LNAI 14523, pp. 59–73, 2024.
https://doi.org/10.1007/978-3-031-57963-9_5

addition, the popularity of these tools has fostered the development of a myriad of other generative models such as MidJourney, Stable Diffusion or Leonardo AI for image generation [36], and LLaMA, Alpaca or Bard for natural language generation [8]. The rapid progress and adoption of these tools indicates that this is only the beginning of an era where generative models will play an instrumental role in content creation.

A fundamental element for the continuous improvement of AI models is the use of massive training datasets from which complex models can be trained. For example, image-generation models currently rely on datasets like LAION5B which has more than five billion captioned images [25], while language models use even larger datasets [17,18]. The availability of a large amount of high-quality training data is one of the major challenges in the training of accurate machine learning models [2]. For text and images, the data is in many cases extracted from the Internet with crawlers that automatically collect billions of images and texts [18,26].

In the near future, when new datasets are constructed by crawling the Internet, many of the images or text downloaded will have been created by generative AI tools. This means that the new training sets will be most likely significantly different from the ones we have today. It can be argued that AI-generated content could be identified and removed from the training dataset. However, this does not seem to be straightforward [3] and may get harder as more and more generative AI models become available. Therefore, it seems likely that future generative AI models will be trained with data generated from previous AI models. In short, there will be a feedback loop where AI-generated content is used to train the next AI models that will in turn generate data used in the training of the following AI models and so on.

This opens a number of questions on how this may impact the evolution of generative AI models. On the one hand, using artificially generated samples for training can be beneficial and is indeed used in some applications where real training data is scarce [6] while on the other hand, it can also lead to degradation. In our case, the situation is much more complex as there will be a mixture of real and AI-generated data and also a feedback loop that can lead to more subtle effects over time. Indeed feedback loops are well known in control theory to be prone to amplify undesired effects and cause unstable behaviour that can lead to the collapse of a system in the long run [5]. This has already been observed on the Internet with Recommender systems [13,20] and the same could occur for generative AI.

One possibility could be to try to break the loop and avoid using AI-generated data when training newer AI models. However, this would require tools that are capable of detecting AI-generated content something that seems challenging. Even if in some cases, it may be viable to detect the content generated by a given AI model [3], there are a myriad of tools and models that generate content and many more are coming. Therefore, it would be playing cat and mouse continuously. Moreover, AI-generated content can also be manipulated or combined, for example, AI-generated images may subsequently be edited making the detection even more complex. Therefore, it seems reasonable to assume that AI-generated content will be present in future massive training datasets extracted from the Internet.

The potential issues of the feedback loop can be illustrated with a few simple cases. For example, many AI image generators, at least on their first versions, were unable to reproduce some elements, like the hands of persons, and created distorted or unnatural hands. If those images were used to train a newer model, would the model tend to reproduce the errors on the hands even if the newer model was now capable of drawing realistic hands? More generally, will the biases or limitations of previous AI models become a burden for newer models? Similarly, it is interesting to see if generative AI models can capture the diversity of the dataset they were trained with or if they can only generate a subset of those patterns thus creating less diverse content. If this does happen, will this be accumulative or stop at some point in time? Conversely, as the AI models evolve, would the generated content resemble the original dataset, will fidelity be gradually lost as part of the evolution? These are just a few open questions of the potential implications of the feedback loop created by using training datasets taken from the Internet.

In this article, we try to gain some initial understanding of this interplay between generative AI models and the Internet extending the preliminary investigation conducted in [21]. In more detail, we use AI image generators and a few simple datasets to model the interactions and run different experiments to evaluate how the AI generators could evolve over time. In doing so, we assume a worst case in which the training set for a given version of the AI tool is generated entirely by the previous version of the AI tool. This allows us to amplify the effects of the interaction. Then the generated images for each version are evaluated in terms of fidelity and diversity compared to the original dataset. The simulation results show how for several datasets diversity and fidelity degrade over time while for others, there is an initial degradation followed by a stabilization. The rest of this article is organised as follows: Sect. 2 reviews diffusion models for image generation and the metrics used for evaluating AI-generated images. Section 3 overviews the methodology and datasets used for the simulation experiments conducted, which are shown in Sect. 4. Related work is discussed in Sect. 5. Finally, Sect. 6 concludes this work with a main summary of its findings and conclusions.

2   Preliminaries

Generative models differ from classical discriminators or classifiers as their goal is to estimate the probability distribution from a set of samples so as to be able to generate samples that correspond approximately to that distribution. Generative models are not only applied to images but also to other complex data formats such as audio, 3D images, or even chemical molecules [19]. Diffusion models represent one class of generative models alongside other architectures that tried to achieve the same goals, like Variational Autoencoders (VAEs) [34] and Generative Adversarial Networks (GANs) [7], however the latter are still competing with diffusion models in quality.

2.1   Diffusion Models

Diffusion models [11,23] are the state-of-the-art architecture of generative models that have achieved unprecedented milestones in generation quality and diversity that previous models could not achieve. They represent a general architecture with a variety of different variations available, however, all are based on two phases: the forward phase and the backward phase. During the first phase, the model gradually introduces Gaussian noise into the images until they degrade to random noise. In the second phase, the model tries to reverse the process. In other words, the model learns how to remove the noise of the image, going from an image of random noise (it can be seen as a random seed) to the real image by gradual steps, removing some noise in each step. To learn this task, the model is trained using the data that has been generated in the first phase, so that it can then be applied during inference.

The first process can be intuitively understood as the preparation of the dataset so that the neural network can learn how to turn the process around [15,32]. This can be specified as a Markov chain where each step only depends on the previous one. Therefore we can calculate it as a chain, see Eq. 1, where X_0 is the original image, t is the number of steps taken and X_t is the final image. In each of these steps Gaussian noise is introduced, as can be seen in Eq. 2, where β is the hyperparameter controlling the scale of noise introduced during the process.

$$q(x_{1:T}|x_0) = \prod_{t=1}^{T} q(x_t|x_{t-1}) \tag{1}$$

$$q(x_t|x_{t-1}) = \mathcal{N}(x_t; \sqrt{1-\beta_t}x_{t-1}, \beta_t I) \tag{2}$$

On the other hand, the reverse procedure is a highly complex process where we will use a model to reverse phase 1. This process is also a Markov chain as shown in Eq. 3. The aim is to approximate the inverse conditional probability of the previous process $p_\theta(\mathbf{x}_{t-1}|\mathbf{x}_t)$ using a model defined by Eq. 4, where $\boldsymbol{\mu}_\theta(\mathbf{x}_t, t)$ and $\boldsymbol{\Sigma}_\theta(\mathbf{x}_t, t)$) are the mean and the covariance matrix respectively [15,32].

$$p_\theta(\mathbf{x}_{0:T}) = p(\mathbf{x}_T) \prod_{t=1}^{T} p_\theta(\mathbf{x}_{t-1}|\mathbf{x}_t) \tag{3}$$

$$p_\theta(\mathbf{x}_{t-1}|\mathbf{x}_t) = \mathcal{N}(\mathbf{x}_{t-1}; \boldsymbol{\mu}_\theta(\mathbf{x}_t, t), \boldsymbol{\Sigma}_\theta(\mathbf{x}_t, t)) \tag{4}$$

One of the main problems with diffusion models when compared to previous models was the time needed to generate new data [33]. This is caused by the fact that a Markov process has to be simulated at each generation step, which greatly slows down the process. Several alternatives to this process have emerged to try to speed it up. One of them has been the Diffusion Implicit [29] models that allow replacing it with generative processes other than Markov, which are deterministic and speed up the generation process to a great extent.

2.2   Metrics

In this section, we describe the metrics that we have used to measure the quality of the images generated by the different versions of the generative models. In particular, the metrics try to capture the fidelity of the generated images with respect to the original images and their diversity which represents their ability to cover all the types of images that are present in the original dataset. Most of the conventional metrics to measure the quality of generative AI images rely on the features extracted by the inception model [30] and try to capture the similarity of the generated images to those of the original dataset. However, those features are only relevant for color images of significant size and are not applicable to small black-and-white images, such as those found in the MNIST dataset. Therefore we will use two groups of metrics, one for small images and the other for larger images.

Metrics for Small Images. For small images for which the inception model is not applicable, we will measure the fidelity of the generated images by training a classifier on the original dataset and measuring its accuracy on the generated images for each version. The rationale is that if the generated images are similar to the original ones, the classifier should have good accuracy. Instead, if the generated images deviate from the original ones, the classifier trained with the original dataset will have lower accuracy. On the other hand, to support the previous measure we have used Cross-Entropy. This will allow us to analyse the confidence with which the classifier determines its predictions and therefore the fidelity from another angle. If the classifier is not very sure of the prediction it will spread the confidence values over several classes, increasing the entropy. Otherwise, if it is very sure of the decision, the prediction will have a very low value. Lastly, unfortunately we have not been able to measure diversity in an efficient way with the help of the classifier because it is a more complex measure.

Metrics Based on Inception. There are a number of metrics based on the inception model:

Fréchet Inception Distance (FID): This is the most widely used metric to quantify how similar the images created by a generative model are to those in the training dataset [10]. FID is computed as follows, first a set of synthetic images is generated. Then the inception model [30] is run on both the training real dataset and the synthetic dataset and the features of the model are extracted. The model is widely used due to its strong performance for feature extraction. Once the features are obtained in the feature space of the inception model, we calculate the mean and covariance of the two image distributions (real and synthetic). Finally, we evaluate the distance between the two datasets X and Y using the following equation:

$$d(X,Y) = \|\mu_X - \mu_Y\|^2 + \mathrm{Tr}\left(\Sigma_X + \Sigma_Y - 2\sqrt{\Sigma_X \Sigma_Y}\right) \tag{5}$$

where X is the original dataset and Y is the synthetic dataset.

The lower the FID distance is, the closer the synthetic dataset Y to the real dataset X. This metric will allow us to better analyse the degradation as the comparison is done at the level of features, for example in the flowers dataset: petals, wings, etc. This will tend to capture the main elements perceived by humans.

Precision and Density: These two metrics also capture the fidelity of the generated images and can complement the Fréchet distance Inception as they allow us to analyse other essential areas of the generation models that are not covered by it [16,22]. Fidelity can be defined as the similarity of the generated image distribution to the original. To calculate this, an area formed from the features extracted by the inception model is constructed. Then it is checked the percentage of images contained in each area: Precision is the percentage of generated images contained in the area of the original dataset. The formula for this is shown in Eq. 6. Density is another very close metric, with the advantage that it has protection against outliers. The use of a comparison of the two will give a better picture of the fidelity.

$$\text{Precision} := \frac{1}{M} \sum_{j=1}^{M} 1_{Y_j \in \text{manifold}(X_1,\ldots,X_N)} \tag{6}$$

Recall and Coverage: These two metrics capture the diversity of the generated metrics [16,22]. Diversity can be defined as the capability of the generative model to generate all the different classes or variations that existed in the original dataset. Recall is calculated by the percentage of original images per area of the generated dataset. The formula for this is shown in Eq. 7. Coverage it is a metric very similar to recall with the advantage of being protected to outliers.

$$\text{Recall} := \frac{1}{N} \sum_{i=1}^{N} 1_{X_i \in \text{manifold}(Y_1,\ldots,Y_N)} \tag{7}$$

3   Methodology and Model for Interaction

In this section, we describe the interaction model and the methodology used in the experiments.

3.1   Interaction Model

In our simulations, each version of the generative model is trained with a dataset composed of elements generated with the previous version of the generative AI model. This is illustrated in Fig. 1 for the first generations. In each generation, the size of the training set is the same as the size of the original dataset used for training. This ensures that the training time is similar in each generation.

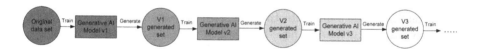

Fig. 1. Interaction model for the evolution of generative AI

This interaction model corresponds to the strongest feedback possible where all the content scraped from the Internet has been generated with the latest version of the generative AI tool. Clearly, this is not realistic as the content on the Internet would be more diverse and include the non-AI generated content and content generated from several generative AI tools and for each of them for several versions. However, considering this strong interaction model allows us to analyze a worst-case scenario that should amplify the effects of the feedback loop and at the same time keep the simulations manageable. The study of more complex interaction models with datasets that grow over time with content generated from different tools and versions is left for future work.

3.2   Methodology

Diffusion Model. For the experiments, we have considered two types of diffusion models: First a diffusion implicit diffusion model for the flowers and Birds dataset experiments to help us with their fast sampling. On the other hand, for the MNIST experiments we have considered using a standard diffusion model with classifier-free diffusion guidance [12] which is one of the most advanced guidance methods.

Datasets. The following datasets have been used in the simulation experiments:

- **MNIST** [4]**:** This is the well-known digit dataset. It contains 60,000 thousand 28 × 28 pixels digit images in black and white.
- **Oxford 102 Flower** [24]**:** This dataset is made up of 8,189 color images of 102 different types of common flowers in the United Kingdom. The flower images have different sizes with most having approximately 700 × 500 pixels. This is a much more complex dataset than MNIST both in terms of image size and number of classes.
- **Caltech-UCSD Birds-200-2011** [31]**:** This is composed of 11,788 color images of 200 different types of birds. The bird images have different sizes with most of them having approximately 500 × 300 pixels. The image complexity is similar to the flowers dataset but with approximately twice the classes.

4   Simulation Experiments and Evaluation

The experiments first use the interaction model described in Sect. 3.1 to create nine generations of the diffusion model and the corresponding datasets. Then the relevant metrics among those discussed in Sect. 2.2 are computed for each generation. The code along with the generated datasets is available at a public repository[1]. The experiments have been run in Google Colab platform using an A100 GPU. The time required to train the diffusion models is the largest part of the computing time and was approximately 90 min for the MNIST and 4 h for the flowers and birds datasets respectively. This section summarizes the results of the experiments analyzing both the quantitative metrics discussed in Sect. 2.2 and also showing some examples of the images generated to visualize the effects.

4.1   MNIST: Guided Diffusion on Simple Datasets

In this first part, we present the results when using a denoising diffusion probabilistic model with a Classifier-Free Diffusion Guidance on the simplest dataset of the ones we consider: MNIST. The simplicity of the images on this dataset combined with a reduced number of classes and the use of guidance should improve the quality of images generated. The influence of the guidance is evaluated using different settings for this parameter. As discussed before, most of the commonly used metrics for generative models can not be used for MNIST as they are based on the Inception model that requires larger color images. Instead, a classifier is trained with the original dataset and then used to evaluate the generated images at each generation. The idea is that if the digits start to deviate significantly from the original ones, the accuracy of the classifier will drop. This would give an indication of the fidelity of the images. Additionally cross-entropy is also used to assess the confidence of the classifier.

Figure 2 summarizes the results, in the top part sample images at different generations are shown while the metrics are placed at the bottom. Three guidance values: 1.0, 0.1, and 1e-10 have been simulated that correspond to strong, weak, and no guidance respectively. It can be observed that guidance, which indicates how closely the generated images are to the desired class, plays a key role in the evolution of the images. When a high guidance value such as 1.0 is used, it can be observed that the digits are well-defined across all the generations, in fact, they tend to be quite similar suggesting a reduction in diversity. Instead, when weaker guidance is used, for example, 0.1, it appears that there is some degeneration in the images but there is no drop in diversity. Finally, for a very low value of guidance, there is a clear degeneration in the output, and the images in some cases do not have a shape that corresponds to any digit.

The accuracy and cross-entropy are also shown at the bottom of Fig. 2. It can be clearly seen that they are consistent with the analysis of the sample images. The accuracy which we use to measure fidelity is stable and close to 100% when

---

[1] https://github.com/gonz-mart/Towards-Understanding-the-Interplay-of-Generative-Artificial-Intelligence-and-the-Internet.

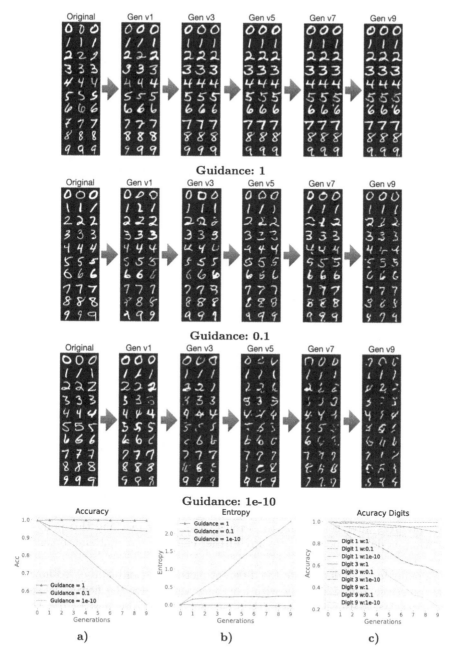

Fig. 2. The top plots show examples of the images generated for the MNIST dataset with different guidance values 1, 0.1, 1e-10 respectively. Plots at the bottom show relevant metrics obtained in the experiments carried out on the previously generated datasets with a classifier. Graph a) shows the results for the accuracy metric. Graph b) shows the results for the entropy and Graph c) provides the accuracy for three digits.

guidance is 1.0. Similarly, cross-entropy is very small which shows that not only the classifier is correct but also that it is confident on its predictions. Instead, for weak guidance, there is a loss in accuracy and a larger cross-entropy over generations suggesting a degradation in the shape of the generated digits. These effects are much more apparent when no guidance is used, in this case, accuracy drops much faster and cross-entropy grows quickly.

Finally, it is interesting to note the importance of the classes in the generation. Part c) of the Figure shows the accuracy of three digits during all the generations, which allows us to see if there has been any difference between the different classes of the data set. As can be seen in the figure, there seems to be clear differences in the degeneration, depending on the level of difficulty of the digit. Simple digits, such as one, have not been affected as much as more complex digits such as three or nine.

4.2   Birds and Flowers: No Guidance on Larger Datasets

In this second part, we present the results when using a diffusion model that has no guidance in the generation when evaluated on relatively complex color images, namely the flowers and birds datasets. A few samples of the images generated with each version of the diffusion model are shown in Fig. 3 for flowers (a) and birds (b). As can be clearly seen, there is a degradation in each iteration of the models, first losing details in the generation, and then ending up in complete noise. After a few versions, the model is not capable of generating images that can be even recognized as flowers or birds. Therefore, in this case, evolution leads to degradation and even collapse. This can also be clearly observed when looking at the quantitative metrics that are also shown in the Figure. The Fréchet Inception Distance (FID) (Fig. 3 (c)) increases with each version, this is consistent with what is visually observed in the figure and shows that for this diffusion model and datasets our interaction model leads to a collapse. However, we have to bear in mind that our interaction model is very strong, and on the Internet, there will be a mixture of images, not just those generated by the previous version of the generative AI tool that we are training. It is important to note that there is no progress after converging to degeneration. After reaching this point, the following models do not generate any further changes and continue to generate this noise.

Looking more in detail into the different metrics, it can be observed how the FID increases, almost linearly with each new version for the flowers while for birds, the degradation is faster in the first generations. This may be due to the birds dataset being more complex than the flowers. This may give us a clue that the degradation may be closely related to the complexity of the dataset and the inability of the model to use it. With the other metrics, the behavior is similar: we can observe how the fidelity and diversity metrics worsen with each iteration until they reach zero. This is seen in (d) for precision and density which measure fidelity and in (e) for recall and coverage which measure diversity.

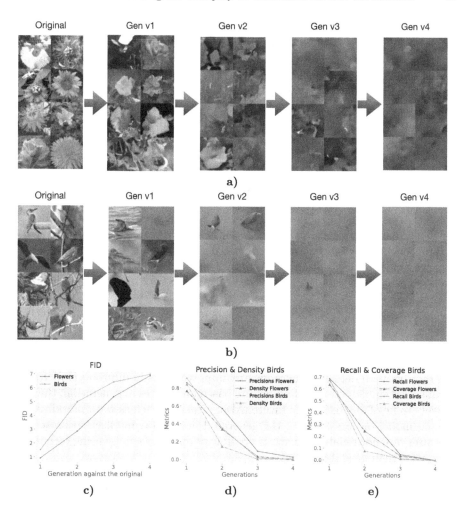

Fig. 3. Subfigures a) and b) show examples of the images generated with each version of the diffusion model of the Oxford 102 Flower [24] and Caltech-UCSD Birds-200-2011 [31] datasets respectively. Subfigures c), d), e) show the results obtained in the experiments carried out on the previous mencioned datasets. Graph a) shows the results of the FID metric. Graphs b) and c) measure respectively Fidelity (precision and density) and Diversity (recall and coverage).

5   Related Work

The first work to be highlighted is the work of Hataya et al. [9], which inspired this paper and measured for the first time the possible consequences if future data sets were to be contaminated with synthetic images. His conclusions are unambiguous about the fact that only the inclusion of these synthetic images could lead to a deterioration of the quality of the data set, incapacitating the model in different tasks. As we have shown in our work. This deterioration is not only maintained but will increase in the future, so if we are not careful with the curation of the data set, this problem will be even bigger in the future. Furthermore, it is interesting to mention that this problem in datasets is not limited to these image generation models, but can also occur in other formats such as text. This has been widely studied [28] knowing that all text that has been generated is detrimental to future models and should be avoided at all costs.

Another interesting line that we have not been able to experiment on is the bias in generation and what impact this constant generation may have. Pathways in generation is a problem that has been investigated a lot because it can lead to race, age, gender and other discriminations, and increase them over time. However, this type of generated data is not always a problem, but can also be beneficial. An example of this is how recently some research is proposing the use of diffusion models to generate synthetic data as augmentation techniques to improve model generalisation [1]. Another similar study also points in the same direction as it is the case that they use a fully synthetic data being and it proves its performance.

On the other hand, it is necessary to talk about all the work on the detection of these generated images, as it will be one of the necessary methods to maintain the quality of the datasets. If we are not able to detect these images, there will be no way to know for sure that our data samples are real. As it stands, we are in a race between detection methods and improvements in diffusion models [35]. Because certain detection techniques are based on failures in generation, they are unlikely to be of any use in the future. Also, measures such as watermarking that allowed model owners to mark the generated images (as intellectual protection measures) are not reliable, since it is possible to disable them by using techniques to prevent their readability [14].

The previously discussed works do not consider the feedback loop that can lead to accumulative effects over time. To the best of our knowledge, we were the first to investigate this issue in [21] showing degeneration for diffusion models over generations. This paper extends our previous analysis by covering additional diffusion models and datasets as well as incorporating quantitative metrics. Recent work has followed our initial steps and considered the problem of interaction between generative models and the Internet presenting some theoretical intuition for some simple models on the causes of degeneration as well as its evaluation for natural language processing generative models [27]. This work complements ours and shows that the feedback can create issues in a wide range of generative models.

6   Conclusions

In this work, we have studied the interaction of generative AI models with the Internet. As AI-generated data populates the Internet it will be part of the training sets for future versions of generative AI creating a feedback loop that can have undesired effects over time. In this paper, these potential effects have been evaluated using a simple interaction model and several generative diffusion models and datasets. The results show that the interaction can lead to degeneration and also to loss of diversity. Although the results are based on a simple interaction model that should be a worst-case for feedback, it confirms that the interaction should be carefully studied to understand its implications. This work is just a step towards understanding of the implications of the interaction between generative AI and the Internet. Additional research is needed with more complex and realistic interaction models that use training sets with a mixture of data generated with different AI models and real data. Similarly, the evaluation using more complex generative AI models and well as additional datasets is required to get a better understanding of the long-term effects of the interaction.

Acknowledgements. This work was supported by the FUN4DATE (PID2022-136684O7B-C21/22) and ENTRUDIT (TED2021-130118B-I00) projects funded by the Spanish Agencia Estatal de Investigacion (AEI).

References

1. Azizi, S., Kornblith, S., Saharia, C., Norouzi, M., Fleet, D.J.: Synthetic data from diffusion models improves imagenet classification. arXiv preprint arXiv:2304.08466 (2023)
2. Bansal, M.A., Sharma, D.R., Kathuria, D.M.: A systematic review on data scarcity problem in deep learning: solution and applications. ACM Comput. Surv. **54**(10s) (2022). https://doi.org/10.1145/3502287
3. Corvi, R., Cozzolino, D., Poggi, G., Nagano, K., Verdoliva, L.: Intriguing properties of synthetic images: from generative adversarial networks to diffusion models (2023)
4. Deng, L.: The MNIST database of handwritten digit images for machine learning research. IEEE Signal Process. Mag. **29**(6), 141–142 (2012)
5. Doyle, J.C., Francis, B.A., Tannenbaum, A.R.: Feedback Control Theory. Courier Corporation, Chelmsford (2013)
6. Fahimi, F., Dosen, S., Ang, K.K., Mrachacz-Kersting, N., Guan, C.: Generative adversarial networks-based data augmentation for brain-computer interface. IEEE Trans. Neural Netw. Learn. Syst. **32**(9), 4039–4051 (2021). https://doi.org/10.1109/TNNLS.2020.3016666
7. Fournaris, A.P., Lalos, A.S., Serpanos, D.: Generative adversarial networks in AI-enabled safety-critical systems: friend or foe? Computer **52**(9), 78–81 (2019). https://doi.org/10.1109/MC.2019.2924546
8. Gozalo-Brizuela, R., Garrido-Merchan, E.C.: ChatGPT is not all you need. a state of the art review of large generative AI models. arXiv (2023). https://doi.org/10.48550/ARXIV.2301.04655, https://arxiv.org/abs/2301.04655
9. Hataya, R., Bao, H., Arai, H.: Will large-scale generative models corrupt future datasets? arXiv preprint arXiv:2211.08095 (2022)
10. Heusel, M., Ramsauer, H., Unterthiner, T., Nessler, B., Hochreiter, S.: GANs trained by a two time-scale update rule converge to a local Nash equilibrium. In: Guyon, I., et al. (eds.) Advances in Neural Information Processing Systems, vol. 30. Curran Associates, Inc. (2017)

11. Ho, J., Jain, A., Abbeel, P.: Denoising diffusion probabilistic models. Adv. Neural Inf. Process. Syst. **33**, 6840–6851 (2020)
12. Ho, J., Salimans, T.: Classifier-free diffusion guidance. arXiv preprint arXiv:2207.12598 (2022)
13. Jiang, R., Chiappa, S., Lattimore, T., György, A., Kohli, P.: Degenerate feedback loops in recommender systems. In: Proceedings of the 2019 AAAI/ACM Conference on AI, Ethics, and Society, pp. 383–390, January 2019.https://doi.org/10.1145/3306618.3314288
14. Jiang, Z., Zhang, J., Gong, N.Z.: Evading watermark based detection of AI-generated content. arXiv preprint arXiv:2305.03807 (2023)
15. Karagiannakos, S., Adaloglou, N.: Diffusion models: toward state-of-the-art image generation (2022). https://theaisummer.com/
16. Kynkäänniemi, T., Karras, T., Laine, S., Lehtinen, J., Aila, T.: Improved precision and recall metric for assessing generative models. Adv. Neural Inf. Process. Syst. **32** (2019)
17. Laurençon, H., et al.: The bigscience roots corpus: a 1.6 TB composite multilingual dataset. In: Koyejo, S., Mohamed, S., Agarwal, A., Belgrave, D., Cho, K., Oh, A. (eds.) Advances in Neural Information Processing Systems, vol. 35, pp. 31809–31826. Curran Associates, Inc. (2022)
18. Lhoest, Q., et al.: Datasets: a community library for natural language processing. In: Proceedings of the 2021 Conference on Empirical Methods in Natural Language Processing: System Demonstrations, pp. 175–184. Association for Computational Linguistics, Online and Punta Cana, Dominican Republic, November 2021.https://doi.org/10.18653/v1/2021.emnlp-demo.21, https://aclanthology.org/2021.emnlp-demo.21
19. Li, C., et al.: Geometry-based molecular generation with deep constrained variational autoencoder. IEEE Trans. Neural Netw. Learn. Syst. 1–10 (2022).https://doi.org/10.1109/TNNLS.2022.3147790
20. Mansoury, M., Abdollahpouri, H., Pechenizkiy, M., Mobasher, B., Burke, R.: Feedback loop and bias amplification in recommender systems. In: Proceedings of the 29th ACM International Conference on Information & Knowledge Management, pp. 2145–2148 (2020)
21. Martínez, G., Watson, L., Reviriego, P., Hernández, J.A., Juarez, M., Sarkar, R.: Combining generative artificial intelligence (AI) and the internet: heading towards evolution or degradation? (2023)
22. Naeem, M.F., Oh, S.J., Uh, Y., Choi, Y., Yoo, J.: Reliable fidelity and diversity metrics for generative models. In: International Conference on Machine Learning, pp. 7176–7185. PMLR (2020)
23. Nichol, A.Q., Dhariwal, P.: Improved denoising diffusion probabilistic models. In: International Conference on Machine Learning, pp. 8162–8171. PMLR (2021)
24. Nilsback, M.E., Zisserman, A.: Automated flower classification over a large number of classes. In: Proceedings of the Indian Conference on Computer Vision, Graphics and Image Processing, December 2008
25. Schuhmann, C., et al.: LAION-5B: an open large-scale dataset for training next generation image-text models. arXiv (2022). https://doi.org/10.48550/ARXIV.2210.08402, https://arxiv.org/abs/2210.08402
26. Schuhmann, C., et al.: LAION-400M: open dataset of CLIP-filtered 400 million image-text pairs. arXiv (2021). https://doi.org/10.48550/ARXIV.2111.02114, https://arxiv.org/abs/2111.02114
27. Shumailov, I., Shumaylov, Z., Zhao, Y., Gal, Y., Papernot, N., Anderson, R.: The curse of recursion: training on generated data makes models forget (2023)

28. Simard, M.: Clean data for training statistical MT: the case of MT contamination. In: Proceedings of the 11th Conference of the Association for Machine Translation in the Americas: MT Researchers Track, pp. 69–82 (2014)
29. Song, J., Meng, C., Ermon, S.: Denoising diffusion implicit models. arXiv preprint arXiv:2010.02502 (2020)
30. Szegedy, C., et al.: Going deeper with convolutions. In: 2015 IEEE Conference on Computer Vision and Pattern Recognition (CVPR), pp. 1–9 (2015). https://doi.org/10.1109/CVPR.2015.7298594
31. Wah, C., Branson, S., Welinder, P., Perona, P., Belongie, S.: Caltech-UCSD birds-200-2011 (cub-200-2011). Technical report. CNS-TR-2011-001, California Institute of Technology (2011)
32. Weng, L.: What are diffusion models? lilianweng.github.io, July 2021. https://lilianweng.github.io/posts/2021-07-11-diffusion-models/
33. Xiao, Z., Kreis, K., Vahdat, A.: Tackling the generative learning trilemma with denoising diffusion GANs. arXiv preprint arXiv:2112.07804 (2021)
34. Zhang, C., Geng, Y., Han, Z., Liu, Y., Fu, H., Hu, Q.: Autoencoder in autoencoder networks. IEEE Trans. Neural Netw. Learn. Syst. 1–13 (2022). https://doi.org/10.1109/TNNLS.2022.3189239
35. Zhang, C., Zhang, C., Zhang, M., Kweon, I.S.: Text-to-image diffusion model in generative AI: a survey. arXiv preprint arXiv:2303.07909 (2023)
36. Zhang, C., Zhang, C., Zhang, M., Kweon, I.S.: Text-to-image diffusion models in generative AI: a survey (2023)

Optimizing Brain Tumor Classification: A Comprehensive Study on Transfer Learning and Imbalance Handling in Deep Learning Models

Raza Imam[1,3(✉)] and Mohammed Talha Alam[2,3]

[1] Aligarh Muslim University, Aligarh, India
[2] Jamia Hamdard University, New Delhi, India
[3] Mohamed Bin Zayed University of Artificial Intelligence, Abu Dhabi, UAE
{raza.imam,mohammed.alam}@mbzuai.ac.ae

Abstract. Deep learning has emerged as a prominent field in recent literature, showcasing the introduction of models that utilize transfer learning to achieve remarkable accuracies in the classification of brain tumor MRI images. However, the majority of these proposals primarily focus on balanced datasets, neglecting the inherent data imbalance present in real-world scenarios. Consequently, there is a pressing need for approaches that not only address the data imbalance but also prioritize precise classification of brain cancer. In this work, we present a novel deep learning-based approach, called Transfer Learning-CNN, for brain tumor classification using MRI data. The proposed model leverages the predictive capabilities of existing publicly available models by utilizing their pre-trained weights and transferring those weights to the CNN. By leveraging a publicly available Brain MRI dataset, the experiment evaluated various transfer learning models for classifying different tumor types, including meningioma, glioma, and pituitary tumors. We investigate the impact of different loss functions, including focal loss, and oversampling methods, such as SMOTE and ADASYN, in addressing the data imbalance issue. Notably, the proposed strategy, which combines VGG-16 and CNN, achieved an impressive accuracy rate of 96%, surpassing alternative approaches significantly. Our code is available at Github.

1 Introduction

Impactful solutions are being offered by the context-aware deployment of deep learning methodologies to enhance medical diagnostics. The World Health Organization (WHO) states that a correct diagnosis of a brain tumor entails its discovery, localization, and classification based on its degree, kind, and severity. This research comprises finding the tumor, grading it according to type and location, and classifying it according to grade in the diagnosis of brain tumors using magnetic resonance imaging (MRI). This approach has experimented with using several models rather than a single model for classification task in order to

F. Cuzzolin and M. Sultana (Eds.): Epi UAI 2023, LNAI 14523, pp. 74–88, 2024.
https://doi.org/10.1007/978-3-031-57963-9_6

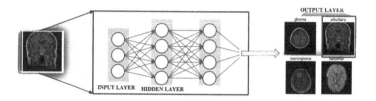

Fig. 1. Conventional Classification of Brain Tumors from MRI images using Convolutional Neural Networks

categorize brain MRI data [15]. Deep learning and transfer learning models have been proposed with higher accuracies in recent literature for classifying Brain Tumor MRI images. However most of such proposals are focused on balanced data. Hence, approaches to account for the imbalance in data, as well as focusing on the precise classification of brain cancer in real world scenarios, are needed. We introduce a 'Transfer Learning + CNN model' rather of just 'Transfer Learning model with Fine Tuning' and compared 8 of such Transfer Learning models using various approaches on imbalance MRI images [12].

Using three pathogenic forms of brain tumor (glioma, meningioma, and pituitary tumor), we aim to propose an accurate and automated classification scheme in this work. Towards this classification task, our goal is to empirically assess how well the most common benchmark models perform. Our goal of offering the finest classification model will open up new research directions in terms of choosing the right model for real-world brain tumor classification deployment. Utilizing tested models, the acquired characteristics are classified. The approach of our experiments that we will be acquiring is also represented in Fig. 1. Subsequently, a thorough assessment of the suggested system is performed utilizing several effective evaluation metrics of classification tasks along with comparing several analytical factors, such as how well each model performs with less training samples from practicality aspect and how overfitting with lower training samples affects performance of the classifier.

1.1 Motivation

Early brain tumor identification and classification represent a significant area of research in the field of medical imaging. It helps in choosing the most appropriate line of action for treatments to save patients' lives. In both children and adults, brain tumors are regarded as one of the most severe disorders. Brain tumors account for 85% to 90% of all major malignancies of the Central Nervous System (CNS). An estimated 11,700 people receive a brain tumor diagnosis each year. For those with a malignant brain or CNS tumor, the 5-year survival rate is around 34% for males and 36% for women [16]. It is difficult to treat brain tumors as we know that our brain has a very complex structure having tissues that are linked to each other in a complex manner. Often, producing MRI results is very difficult and time-consuming in underdeveloped nations due to a shortage of skilled medical professionals and a lack of understanding of malignancies.

Depending on the tumor's severity-that is, its location, size, and type-different treatment methods are possible. The most common technique for treating brain tumors at the moment is surgery since it has no adverse implications on the brain. There are different medical imaging techniques that are used to view the internal structures of a human body in order to discover any abnormalities [9]. The most often used of them to identify brain tumors is Magnetic Resonance Imaging (MRI) since it can show abnormalities that may not be seen or just dimly visible on computed tomography (CT) [11]. However, the rush of patients makes it difficult, chaotic, and perhaps error-prone to manually review these images. Automated classification methods based on machine learning and artificial intelligence have regularly outperformed manual classification in terms of accuracy in order to solve such issues. Therefore, recommending a system that does detection and classification utilizing deep learning algorithms employing the above-mentioned benchmark models would be helpful for radiologists and other medical professionals.

1.2 Contributions

In this work, we focus on imbalance problem of Brain Tumor Classification as it is a real-world scenario in deployment. To solve this imbalance problem, we experiment with several loss functions including focal loss. Along with this, a comparative study is conducted on the performance of different oversampling methods including augmentation, SMOTE, and ADASYN. The models are experimented on are 8 Transfer Learning-CNN models that incorporates the base Transfer learning model, followed by the integration of proposed CNN layers. Following a detailed evaluation of each Transfer Learning-CNN model, we finally conclude VGG16-CNN is the novel proposal of this study.

- Developed a Transfer learning-CNN framework for brain tumor MRI classification, utilizing pre-trained models, where the produced weights transfer to an 8-layer CNN head for effective training.
- Employed 8 different transfer learning models integrated with CNNs to increase the classification accuracy on different types of brain cancer (no tumor, glioma, meningioma, and pituitary cancer).
- Experimented with 5 different approaches to deal with imbalanced datasets such as- Changing loss functions: (1) Focal loss (2) Cross Entropy, and Oversampling methods: (3) Data Augmentation, (4) SMOTE (5) ADASYN.
- Assessed empirical evaluation of the models under the different approaches on metrics including Accuracy, Precision, Recall, and F1 Score.

2   Related Works

The classification of brain tumors using MRI data has been the subject of numerous studies based on convolutional neural networks in recent years. Many of these methods make use of hybrid approaches, and many also offer technical

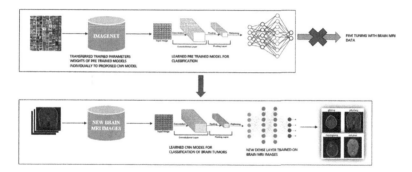

Fig. 2. Traditional Transfer Learning vs Transfer Learning-CNN

variations on widely used deep learning models [3]. In [6], the authors describe a classification method for the 3-class classification issue that combines transfer learning with GoogleNets. They used a number of evaluation metrics, with a mean classification accuracy of 98%, including area under the curve (AUC), precision, recall, F-score, and specificity. [1] have made use of the benefit of differential CNN by generating extra differential feature maps. With the capacity to categorize a sizable database of pictures with high accuracy of about 98%, their approach demonstrated a considerable improvement for the brain MRI classification problem. In [14], the authors proposed a hybrid architecture by adopting GoogleNet as a based CNN model while tweaking the last few layers for the specific Brain Tumor Classification. Their proposal attained the classification accuracy of 99.67%. Moreover, [10] conducted a multi-class study of Brain Tumor MRI Images as they propose a CNN model for early diagnoses purposes with fully optimized framework. Compared to the conventional CNN models, their solution attained an accuracy of 98.14% (Fig. 2).

3 Methodology

3.1 Transfer Learning and CNN

We observed that using the most recent transfer learning models that have been presented in the most recent literature produced relatively decent results when trained on the balanced Brain MRI datasets. This empirical evaluation of brain tumor classification is focused on the Imbalance problem. However, in training such Transfer Learning models with fine tuning on the imbalance dataset did not show as good results in comparison to the Transfer models integrated with newly added CNN layers [12]. Since the later case demonstrated improved predicted accuracies on the unbalanced dataset, we experiment with 8 of these Transfer Learning models that are combined with newly added CNN layers. The ImageNet training dataset was used to train the traditional pre-train models, namely VGG16, EfficientNetB0, EfficientNetB3, ResNet50, DenseNet201, MobileNet, GoogleNet, XceptionNet. For effective training, each model's trained

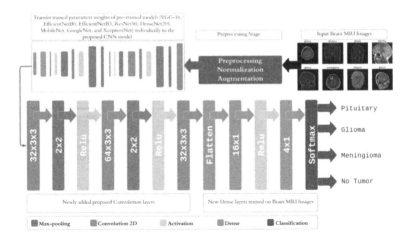

Fig. 3. The proposed framework for the classification of brain tumor MRIs. Here, the pre-trained CNN models (VGG16-CNN, EfficientNetB0-CNN, EfficientNetB3-CNN, ResNet50-CNN, DenseNet201-CNN, MobileNet-CNN, GoogleNet-CNN, and XceptionNet-CNN) are trained using the Imagenet dataset, and the produced weights of these pre-trained models are individually transferred to the suggested CNN model for effective training

parameter weights were transferred to the newly added layers of the additional CNN model. The CNN model was then fine-tuned using the brain tumor augmented MRI data set for final classification into 4 classes. CNN, VGG16-CNN, EfficientNetB0-CNN, EfficientNetB3-CNN, ResNet50-CNN, DenseNet201-CNN, MobileNet-CNN, GoogleNet-CNN, XceptionNet-CNN are the resultant models we empirically evaluated the training performance on the imbalanced dataset using various approaches.

3.2   Proposed Method

The proposed Transfer Learning-CNN (VGG-CNN) model incorporates the base Transfer learning model, i.e., VGG16, followed by the basic structure of the CNNs. It might take days to weeks to train a raw CNN completely from scratch, making it a difficult task [14]. Therefore, it would be preferable to train the suggested deep learning approach using a pre-trained classifier rather than creating a new deep learning classifier from start [13]. Additionally, in terms of predictive accuracy, our Transfer Learning models combined with CNN performed significantly better on the imbalanced Brain MRI dataset than the base CNN as well as the base Transfer Learning model with Fine tuning. In order to do this, we chose the most accurate current Transfer Learning model on the balanced dataset, VGG16, as our foundation model. CNN architecture VGG16 was employed to win the 2014 ILSVR (Imagenet) competition. It is regarded as one of the best vision model architectures created to date. The most distinctive feature of VGG16 is that it prioritized having convolution layers of 3 × 3 filters with a stride 1 and always utilized the same padding and maxpool layer of 2 × 2 filters with a stride 2. Throughout the entire architecture, convolution and max pool layers are arranged in the same manner. It concludes with two fully connected layers (FC) and a softmax for output.

Moreover, the final four layers of VGG-16 were dropped from the planned VGG-CNN architecture, and 8 new levels were added in their place. After these adjustments, there were 148 layers overall instead of 144. Addition to the layers of transfer learning model, the first convolution layer of the CNN portion, uses a filter size of 3 × 3 with the depth of 32, which immediately reduces the image size followed by a max pooling layer of 2 × 2 filter. The second convolution layer has a depth of 64 with the same filter size of 3 × 3, followed by a max pooling layer of 2 × 2 filter. Again, a 2D convolution layer of depth 32 with filter size 3 × 3 is incorporated followed by a Flatten layer. Dense layer of 16 hidden units with relu activation and the final output layer of 4 units with softmax activation are used. Compared to the initial 4 layers of transfer learning models, adding the extra convolutional layers in the CNN portion gave us more detailed, accurate, and robust features. These 3 later convolutional layers extracted high-level features compared with the initial layer, which extracted low-level features. The choice of this additional 8-layer architecture as the head on the pre-trained network was based on several considerations. We aimed to strike a balance between model complexity and performance. This 8-layer architecture was found to be effective in capturing the necessary features for our specific task, while not being overly complex, which could lead to overfitting or increased computational requirements. Our method's superior robustness is supported by evaluating various architectures during experimentation, where the 8-layer head consistently demonstrated better performance across multiple metrics and outperformed other architectures in diverse datasets and scenarios. Hence, compared to the traditional Transfer learning model, the proposed Transfer Learning-CNN model achieves higher accuracies in comparison as more intricate, exclusionary, and deep features have been acquired in the proposed method. The specific architecture of the proposed methodology is also shown in Fig. 3.

3.3   Experiments

The experiments have been performed on a combination of three distinct datasets taken from Kaggle namely figshare, SARTAJ and Br35H. This accumulated custom imbalance dataset contains about 4200 images of human brain MRI images which are classified into 4 classes: no-tumor (1760), glioma (858), meningioma (1265) and pituitary (341) cancer, whereas no-tumor class images were taken from the Br35H dataset. The dataset images have been normalized and resized as a part of pre-processing according to the input size of the proposed model, i.e., 128 × 128. In addition, the accumulated dataset is divided into train and test with 90:10 ratio for validation purpose. The results mentioned in this study only apply to the test set. The testing dataset is then used to evaluate all of the

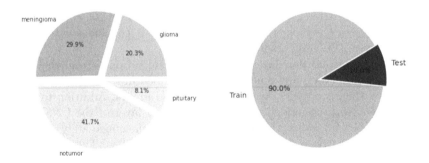

Fig. 4. Data distribution of different classes for imbalanced Brain MRI dataset (Left). Train-Test split (Right)

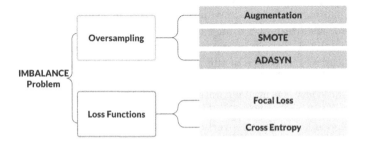

Fig. 5. Distribution of the incorporated approaches to resolve data imbalance

predictive metric claims made about the models in the results and discussion section (Fig. 4).

Predictive modeling is challenged by imbalanced classifications because the majority of machine learning methods for classification were devised on the premise that there should be a similar number of samples in each category. The distribution of examples among the recognized classes is skewed or biased in imbalance classes. These kind of issues with a strong to weak bias in the dataset are typical in real-world applications. As a result of such imbalance, models perform poorly in terms of prediction, particularly for the minority class [6,7]. This is a complication since, in general, the minority class is more significant and, as a result, the issue is more susceptible to errors in classifying for the minority class than the classes with the higher samples. In the real-world scenarios of a model deployment, imbalanced classification is a huge complication [4]. Hence, in our experiments, we tried to empirically evaluate majority of the existing solutions that can be used for imbalanced or long tail classification problems (Figs. 5 and 6).

Focal Loss and Cross Entropy. For each of the 8 deep learning models, we comparatively examined 5 distinct approaches on each of them in order

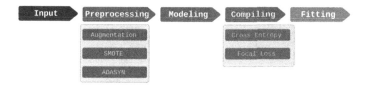

Fig. 6. Implementation of data imbalance approaches

to address the imbalance scenarios that arise during the classification of brain tumors. We explore with changing the loss function in our modeling because it's one of the main reasons that simple examples will divert training in an unbalanced class scenario. We compared the results of test accuracy on our models by changing Cross Entropy with Focal loss in order to obtain better results. Focal Loss, one of the effective solutions in terms of loss functions, deals with this imbalance issue and is created in a way that allows the network to concentrate on training the challenging cases by lowering the loss (or "down-weight") for the simple examples. In other words, Focal loss reduces the importance of the simple examples and emphasizes the difficult ones; thus, smaller class counts would have heavier weights in errors than cross-entropy. The Cross-Entropy loss is multiplied by a modifying factor in focal loss [5]. When a sample is incorrectly classified, the modulating factor is close to 1, p is low, and the loss is unchanged. The modulating factor gets closer to zero as p approaches 1 and the loss for correctly categorized samples gets down-weighted.

$$FL(P_t) = -\alpha_t(1 - P_t)^\gamma log(P_t)$$

Here, P_t = P if $\gamma = 1$, else (1-P); where $\gamma = 0$, $\alpha_t = 1$ then FL is Cross Entropy Loss. In addition, oversampling, which uses artificial data creation to increase the number of samples in the data set, is one of the most fundamental approaches in the state of the art to handle the imbalance problem, other than loss functions [17]. By producing synthetic observations based on the minority observations already there, oversampling aims to grow the minority class so that the data set becomes balanced. In our experimental evaluations, we used 3 oversampling approaches, namely Augmentation, SMOTE, and ADASYN methods.

Data Augmentation. Data augmentation is used to expand the volume of data by introducing slightly altered versions of either existing data or brand-new synthetic data that is derived from available data. It also serves as a regularization term and aids in lowering overfitting when a model is being trained [10]. In our experiments, we tried to augment the samples from minority classes to achieve the number of the samples equal to the majority class. The augmentation tasks we applied to such minority class samples are brightness, contrast, and sharpness alteration each with a random intensity of 80% to 120%. This was followed by the normalization process as a part of preprocessing.

SMOTE. Second oversampling method we implemented on our dataset was SMOTE (Synthetic Minority Oversampling Technique). By creating artificial

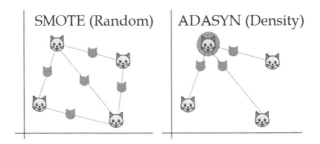

Fig. 7. Working of SMOTE vs ADASYN algorithm

data samples that are marginally different from the current data points on the basis of the existing data points, SMOTE performs oversampling. Following is how the SMOTE algorithm operates:

- A random sample is picked from the minority class.
- Locate the k nearest neighbors for the observations in this minority class sample.
- The vector (line) between the existing data point and one of those neighbors will then be determined using that neighbor.
- The vector is then multiplied by a randomized range unit between 0 and 1.
- We combine this with the existing data point to get the synthetic data sample in the space.

ADASYN. ADASYN is an improvised version of SMOTE. It accomplishes the same things as SMOTE, albeit slightly better. It then adds a random tiny value to the points to make it more realistic after creating those synthetic samples [14]. In other words, the sample's variance, or degree of dispersion, is a little higher than its linear correlation to the parent. Moreover, ADASYN adaptively change the weights of different minority samples to compensate for the skewed distributions. Difference between SMOTE and ADASYN oversampling approaches is also shown in Fig. 7.

We examined each of our 8 TL-CNN models on each of these above-mentioned 5 approaches - Focal Loss, Cross Entropy, Data Augmentation, SMOTE, and ADASYN, with an aim to achieve higher test accuracy on the imbalance dataset. Focal loss is initially compared with the Cross Entropy loss on unbalanced dataset, whereas Data Augmentation, SMOTE, and ADASYN are compared on the unbalanced dataset too but with cross entropy as these later 3 approaches are oversampling approaches [1]. With the parameters listed in Table 1, we conducted tests using a trial-and-error methodology. In order to determine the best convergence for each TL-CNN model, we continuously tracked the development of the training validation accuracy and error. With a mini-batch size of 20 images and an initial learning rate ranging between 0.001 and 0.0001 depending on the model, we utilized mini-batch GD to train the TL-CNN models. To get the results that are explained in the following section, the evaluated models were trained on 5–12 epochs for brain tumor classification.

Table 1. Several parameters utilised during the training phase

Parameter	Values
Mini Batch Size	20
Number of Epochs	5 to 12
Learning Rate(s)	0.001 to 0.0001
Shuffle	True
Steps Per Epoch	Train Size (1600)/20
Dense Activations	RELU
Optimizer	ADAM

3.4 Evaluation

For the typical assessment of a classifier, numerous performance metrics are specified, including Classification Accuracy, Precision, Recall, and F1-Score [2]. The evaluation employs criteria besides the total classification accuracy due to the unbalanced dataset. The mean of correctly classified samples from each class is used to compute balanced accuracy. A class's F-score is determined by taking the harmonic mean of its precision and recall values.

$$\text{Precision} = \frac{\text{True Positive}}{\text{True Positive} + \text{False Positive}}; \quad \text{Recall} = \frac{\text{TP}}{\text{TP} + \text{FN}}$$

$$\text{Accuracy} = \frac{\text{TN} + \text{TP}}{\text{TN} + \text{FP} + \text{TP} + \text{FN}}; \quad F1 \text{ Score} = 2 \times \frac{\text{Precision} \times \text{Recall}}{\text{Precision} + \text{Recall}}$$

When the test dataset has an identical amount of samples from each category, classification accuracy is a useful metric to assess performance. Nevertheless, the dataset we aim to use for this categorization problem under discussion is adequately imbalance. This calls for a more thorough assessment of the suggested system using more evaluation metrics. To evaluate the effectiveness of our tumor categorization method, we employed other metrics including Precision, Recall, and F1-Score. Tables 2, 3, 4, and 5 presents a summary of such metrics on each of the 8 models in terms of various approaches we employed to resolve imbalance classification. The effectiveness of the relevant implemented models that have been implemented in our categorization are empirically evaluated using these classification metrics. Due to the existence of imbalance among the 4 classes, we also showed individual precision values for each class that have been implemented using different approach.

Precision, recall (or sensitivity), and F1-Score are crucial indicators, and they are determined using the relations described above. For each class, the harmonic mean of recall and precision yields the F1-score, another significant statistical classification metric. If we obtain high F1-Score values across all classes, this suggests that we have successfully identified samples free of any class of brain tumor. Due to the existence of imbalance among the 4 classes, we also showed individual precision values for each class that have been implemented using different

Table 2. Evaluation of Integrated frameworks performance on imbalanced dataset when trained with Cross Entropy Loss. The space complexity of each model is the number of trainable parameters. M = Million. The space complexity increases with increasing number of trainable parameters. The time complexity is the training time (in hours) of the models

Model	Space Complexity	Time (hrs) Complexity	LR	Acc.	Precision				Recall				F1 Score			
					P	M	G	NT	P	M	G	NT	P	M	G	NT
CNN	440k	0.091	0.001	0.8125	1.00	0.67	0.73	0.98	0.48	0.91	0.51	0.96	0.65	0.77	0.60	0.97
VGG16-CNN	15.7M	0.26	0.0001	0.83	0.73	0.66	0.94	0.99	0.73	0.66	0.41	1.00	0.60	0.78	0.57	1.00
EfficientNetB0-CNN	4.05M	0.27	0.001	0.37	0.00	0.17	0.00	0.39	0.04	0.04	0.00	0.86	0.00	0.07	0.00	0.54
EfficientNetB3-CNN	10.8M	0.47	1.6e−5	0.60	0.50	0.60	0.38	0.65	0.06	0.46	0.27	0.96	0.11	0.52	0.31	0.78
ResNet50-CNN	23.5M	0.31	0.001	0.78	1.00	0.87	0.60	0.83	0.39	0.59	0.82	0.97	0.56	0.70	0.69	0.90
DenseNet201-CNN	51.8M	0.57	0.001	0.47	0.33	0.43	0.67	0.49	0.23	0.32	0.05	0.82	0.27	0.37	0.10	0.61
MobileNet-CNN	3M	0.126	0.001	0.30	0.00	0.30	0.00	0.00	0.00	1.00	0.00	0.00	0.00	0.46	0.00	0.00
GoogleNet-CNN	6M	0.14	0.0001	0.77	0.71	0.64	0.58	0.97	0.65	0.67	0.56	0.96	0.68	0.65	0.57	0.97
XceptionNet-CNN	25 M	0.15	0.0001	0.83	0.90	0.66	0.89	0.99	0.61	0.95	0.42	0.99	0.73	0.78	0.57	0.99

Table 3. Evaluation of Integrated frameworks performance on imbalanced dataset when trained with Focal Loss

Model	Space Complexity	Time (hrs) Complexity	LR	Acc.	Precision				Recall				F1 Score			
					P	M	G	NT	P	M	G	NT	P	M	G	NT
CNN	440k	0.084	0.001	0.80	0.88	0.68	0.61	0.99	0.45	0.81	0.56	0.98	0.60	0.74	0.59	0.98
VGG16-CNN	15.7M	0.267	0.0001	0.85	0.93	0.68	0.88	1.00	0.87	0.98	0.37	0.98	0.90	0.81	0.52	0.99
EfficientNetB0-CNN	4.05M	0.27	0.001	0.42	0.00	0.00	0.00	0.42	0.00	0.00	0.00	1.00	0.00	0.00	0.00	0.59
EfficientNetB3-CNN	10.8M	0.47	1.6e−5	0.32	0.00	0.22	0.18	0.37	0.00	0.14	0.09	0.62	0.00	0.17	0.12	0.46
ResNet50-CNN	23.5M	0.31	0.001	0.62	0.69	0.45	1.00	0.97	0.71	0.95	0.17	0.59	0.70	0.61	0.29	0.73
DenseNet201-CNN	51.8M	0.57	0.001	0.66	0.57	0.50	0.24	0.96	0.39	0.68	0.15	0.94	0.46	0.58	0.19	0.95
MobileNet-CNN	3M	0.13	0.001	0.42	0.00	0.00	0.00	0.42	0.00	0.00	0.00	1.00	0.00	0.00	0.00	0.59
GoogleNet-CNN	6M	0.14	0.0001	0.78	0.73	0.62	0.74	0.97	0.61	0.88	0.33	0.97	0.67	0.72	0.46	0.97
XceptionNet-CNN	25M	0.20	0.0001	0.81	0.83	0.62	0.84	1.00	0.61	0.92	0.33	1.00	0.70	0.74	0.48	1.00

Table 4. Evaluation of Integrated frameworks performance on imbalanced dataset when trained with SMOTE oversampling

Model	Space Complexity	Time (hrs) Complexity	LR	Acc.	Precision				Recall				F1 Score			
					P	M	G	NT	P	M	G	NT	P	M	G	NT
CNN	440k	0.11	0.001	0.82	0.86	0.71	0.71	0.93	0.77	0.83	0.45	0.99	0.81	0.76	0.55	0.96
VGG16-CNN	15.7M	0.52	0.0001	0.86	0.96	0.71	0.83	0.99	0.81	0.96	0.50	0.97	0.88	0.81	0.62	0.98
EfficientNetB0-CNN	4.05M	0.45	0.001	0.47	0.00	0.38	0.00	0.51	0.00	0.41	0.00	0.82	0.00	0.39	0.00	0.63
EfficientNetB3-CNN	10.8M	1.04	1.6e−5	0.50	0.00	0.39	0.00	0.88	0.00	0.97	0.00	0.51	0.00	0.55	0.00	0.64
ResNet50-CNN	23.5M	0.77	0.001	0.66	1.00	0.97	0.37	0.96	0.19	0.27	0.95	0.89	0.32	0.42	0.54	0.92
DenseNet201-CNN	51.8M	2.08	0.001	0.86	0.96	0.70	0.97	0.99	0.77	0.98	0.45	0.99	0.86	0.82	0.61	0.99
MobileNet-CNN	3M	0.27	0.001	0.42	0.00	0.00	0.00	0.42	0.00	0.00	0.00	1.00	0.00	0.00	0.00	0.59
GoogleNet-CNN	6M	0.14	0.0001	0.79	0.88	0.68	0.57	1.00	0.74	0.66	0.72	0.93	0.81	0.67	0.64	0.96
XceptionNet-CNN	25M	0.27	0.0001	0.83	0.91	0.66	0.82	1.00	0.68	0.94	0.41	0.99	0.78	0.78	0.55	1.00

Table 5. Evaluation of Integrated frameworks performance on imbalanced dataset when trained with ADASYN oversampling

Model	Space Complexity	Time (hrs) Complexity	LR	Acc.	Precision				Recall				F1 Score			
					P	M	G	NT	P	M	G	NT	P	M	G	NT
CNN	440k	0.12	0.001	0.83	0.83	0.75	0.64	0.97	0.77	0.77	0.59	1.00	0.80	0.76	0.61	0.98
VGG16-CNN	15.7M	0.60	0.0001	0.87	0.91	0.75	0.81	1.00	0.94	0.92	0.54	0.99	0.92	0.82	0.65	0.99
EfficientNetB0-CNN	4.05M	0.63	0.001	0.42	0.00	0.00	0.00	0.42	0.00	0.00	0.00	1.00	0.00	0.00	0.00	0.59
EfficientNetB3-CNN	10.8M	1.11	1.6e−5	0.52	1.00	0.36	0.33	0.86	0.13	0.15	0.87	0.69	0.23	0.21	0.48	0.69
ResNet50-CNN	23.5M	0.83	0.001	0.42	0.00	0.00	0.00	0.42	0.00	0.00	0.00	1.00	0.00	0.00	0.00	0.59
DenseNet201-CNN	51.8M	1.67	0.001	0.90	1.00	0.85	0.94	0.85	0.77	0.90	0.76	1.00	0.87	0.87	0.84	0.95
MobileNet-CNN	3M	0.30	0.001	0.42	0.00	0.00	0.00	0.42	0.00	0.00	0.00	1.00	0.00	0.00	0.00	0.59
GoogleNet-CNN	6M	0.15	0.0001	0.77	0.82	0.66	0.49	1.00	0.74	0.58	0.63	0.97	0.78	0.62	0.55	0.98
XceptionNet-CNN	25M	0.31	0.0001	0.86	0.96	0.70	0.90	0.99	0.81	0.97	0.45	0.99	0.88	0.81	0.60	0.99

Table 6. Accuracy Comparison on Unbalanced Dataset using several imbalance solution approaches. The highlighted row indicates the best performing version of our proposed Transfer Learning-CNN approach

Model	CE	Focal Loss	Augment CE	SMOTE CE	ADASYN CE
CNN	0.81	0.80	0.91	0.82	0.83
VGG16-CNN	**0.83**	**0.85**	**0.96**	**0.86**	**0.87**
EfficientNetB0-CNN	0.37	0.42	0.31	0.47	0.42
EfficientNetB3-CNN	0.60	0.32	0.32	0.50	0.52
ResNet50-CNN	0.78	0.62	0.80	0.66	0.42
DenseNet201-CNN	0.47	0.66	0.94	0.86	0.90
MobileNet-CNN	0.30	0.42	0.23	0.42	0.42
GoogleNet-CNN	0.77	0.78	0.80	0.79	0.77
XceptionNet-CNN	0.83	0.81	0.94	0.83	0.86

approach. We also intend to compare several analytical factors, such as how well each model performs with less training samples from practicality aspect and how overfitting with lower training samples affects performance of the classifier.

4 Results and Discussion

This study aimed to appropriately categorize four distinct kind of brain tumor MRI scans. We compared 5 different methodologies-augmentation, focal loss, SMOTE, and ADASYN - while using 8 transfer learning + CNN models. We used a variety of evaluation criteria, including accuracy, precision, recall, and F1-score, to evaluate the effectiveness of our suggested model. This unbalanced dataset was categorized using deep learning models that have already been trained as well as the suggested transfer learning + CNN model, with 90% of the dataset being used for training and 10% being utilized for testing. The performance of deep learning networks for classification can be measured using various methods. In the CNN process, classification tasks are frequently carried out using a confusion matrix. The accuracy comparison on imbalanced dataset utilized in this research is shown in the Table 6.

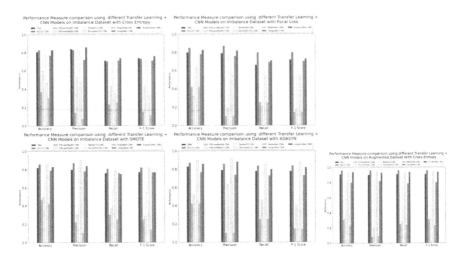

Fig. 8. Performance comparison using various transfer learning models + CNN on different techniques for handling data imbalance

The result of the above experiments showed that VGG-16 performed best overall across all techniques for the accuracy evaluation metric. With augmentation, 0.96 was the highest accuracy ever attained overall. In this instance, MobileNet and EfficientNets had the worst results with an overall accuracy of 0.23 and 0.31, respectively. For the relevant unbalanced dataset on VGG16, EfficientNets, DenseNet201, MobileNet, and GoogleNet, it was found that focal loss obtained higher accuracies than cross entropy loss when the loss functions were compared having values 0.85, 0.66, 0.42 and 0.78, respectively. With the cross-entropy loss, the remaining models fared better. Data augmentation produced the overall best accuracy of the techniques used to address the data imbalance issue.

In all classes where VGG-16 + CNN with data augmentation outperformed other approaches, we computed the average precision, recall, and F1 scores. To summarize, despite having far less layers than other models, transfer learning using the VGG-16 model performed the best overall. The performance measures employing various transfer learning + CNN models on our unbalanced dataset are compared in Fig. 8. Here, we note that performance on an augmented dataset with cross-entropy loss outperforms alternative methods across a range of evaluation parameters.

5   Conclusion and Future Work

Most computer-aided modeling techniques for the investigation of medical image data heavily rely on the CNN model for precise and reliable medical image classification [8]. We have proposed a deep learning-based detection and identification technique for classifying brain tumors in our research study. With the help of brain tumor MRI imaging data, we have examined various transfer learning models for the classification of tumor kinds, including meningioma, glioma, and pituitary. We have added various transfer learning techniques, followed by a CNN model for each method, to improve the CNN model's predictive power. According to the experimental findings, the proposed strategy, which combines VGG-16 and CNN, has a 96% accuracy rate which is significantly higher when compared with other approaches.

The proposed method's notable prediction accuracy was mostly due to data augmentation; further contributing aspects included altering the number of layers, using optimizers, and experimenting with various activation functions. In the future, we will concentrate on optimizing the VGG16 and DenseNet models through rigorous GridSearchCV and hyperparameter tuning, which requires a lot of effort and computing power. We also want to focus on MobileNet due to its simplicity and increased use in real-world settings.

Acknowledgement. We sincerely thank Dr. Rao Anwer, our course advisor at Mohamed Bin Zayed University of Artificial Intelligence, for his invaluable guidance and support throughout this work. Additionally, we extend our special appreciation to Mohamed Bin Zayed University of Artificial Intelligence for providing us with the required computational resources to conduct the experiments featured in this study. Their support has been pivotal in the successful completion of our research.

References

1. Abd El Kader, I., Xu, G., Shuai, Z., Saminu, S., Javaid, I., Salim Ahmad, I.: Differential deep convolutional neural network model for brain tumor classification. Brain Sci. **11**(3), 352 (2021)
2. Alam, M.T., et al.: Its your turn, are you ready to get vaccinated? Towards an exploration of vaccine hesitancy using sentiment analysis of Instagram posts. Mathematics **10**(22) (2022)
3. Alam, M.T., Ubaid, S., Sohail, S.S., Nadeem, M., Hussain, S., Siddiqui, J.: Comparative analysis of machine learning based filtering techniques using movielens dataset. Procedia Comput. Sci. **194**, 210–217 (2021)
4. Badža, M.M., Barjaktarović, M.Č.: Classification of brain tumors from MRI images using a convolutional neural network. Appl. Sci. **10**(6), 1999 (2020)
5. Chatterjee, S., Nizamani, F.A., Nurnberger, A., Speck, O.: Classification of brain tumours in MR images using deep spatiospatial models. Sci. Rep. **12**(1), 1–11 (2022)
6. Deepak, S., Ameer, P.M.: Brain tumor classification using deep CNN features via transfer learning. Comput. Biol. Med. **111**, 103345 (2019)
7. Deepak, S., Ameer, P.M.: Brain tumor categorization from imbalanced MRI dataset using weighted loss and deep feature fusion. Neurocomputing (2022)
8. Imam, R., Huzaifa, M., Azz, M.E.A.: On enhancing the robustness of vision transformers: defensive diffusion (2023)
9. Imam, R., et al.: A systematic literature review of attribute based encryption in health services. J. King Saud Univ. Comput. Inf. Sci. **34**(9), 6743–6774 (2022)
10. Irmak, E.: Multi-classification of brain tumor MRI images using deep convolutional neural network with fully optimized framework. Iran. J. Sci. Technol. Trans. Electr. Eng. **45**(3), 1015–1036 (2021)

11. Kibriya, H., Amin, R., Alshehri, A.H., Masood, M., Alshamrani, S.S., Alshehri, A.: A novel and effective brain tumor classification model using deep feature fusion and famous machine learning classifiers. Comput. Intell. Neurosci. **2022** (2022)

12. Haq, A.U., Li, J.P., Khan, S., Alshara, M.A., Alotaibi, R.M., Mawuli, C., et al.: DACBT: deep learning approach for classification of brain tumors using MRI data in IoT healthcare environment. Sci. Rep. **12**(1), 1–14 (2022)

13. Petmezas, G., et al.: Automated lung sound classification using a hybrid CNN-LSTM network and focal loss function. Sensors **22**(3), 1232 (2022)

14. Raza, A., et al.: A hybrid deep learning-based approach for brain tumor classification. Electronics **11**(7), 1146 (2022)

15. Veeramuthu, A., Kotecha, K., Saini, J.R., Vijayakumar, V., Subramaniyaswamy, V.: MRI brain tumor image classification using a combined feature and image-based classifier. Front. Psychol. **13** (2022)

16. Wang, T., Changhua, L., Yang, M., Hong, F., Liu, C.: A hybrid method for heartbeat classification via convolutional neural networks, multilayer perceptrons and focal loss. PeerJ Comput. Sci. **6**, e324 (2020)

17. Xie, Y., et al.: Convolutional neural network techniques for brain tumor classification (from 2015 to 2022): review, challenges, and future perspectives. Diagnostics **12**(8), 1850 (2022)

Towards Offline Reinforcement Learning with Pessimistic Value Priors

Filippo Valdettaro[1]([✉])[iD] and A. Aldo Faisal[1,2][iD]

[1] Brain and Behaviour Lab, Department of Computing, Imperial College London,
London SW7 2AZ, UK
{filippo.valdettaro20,a.faisal}@imperial.ac.uk
[2] Chair in Digital Health and Data Science, University of Bayreuth,
95447 Bayreuth, Germany

Abstract. Offline reinforcement learning (RL) seeks to train agents in sequential decision-making tasks using only previously collected data and without directly interacting with the environment. As the agent tries to improve on the policy present in the dataset, it can introduce distributional shift between the training data and the suggested agent's policy which can lead to poor performance. To avoid the agent assigning high values to out-of-distribution actions, successful offline RL requires some form of conservatism to be introduced. Here we present a model-free inference framework that encodes this conservatism in the prior belief of the value function: by carrying out policy evaluation with a pessimistic prior, we ensure that only the actions that are directly supported by the offline dataset will be modelled as having a high value. In contrast to other methods, we do not need to introduce heuristic policy constraints, value regularisation or uncertainty penalties to achieve successful offline RL policies in a toy environment. An additional consequence of our work is a principled quantification of Bayesian uncertainty in off-policy returns in model-free RL. While we are able to present an implementation of this framework to verify its behaviour in the exact inference setting with Gaussian processes on a toy problem, the scalability issues that it suffers as the central avenue for further work. We address in more detail these limitations and consider future directions to improve the scalability of this framework beyond the vanilla Gaussian process implementation, proposing a path towards improving offline RL algorithms in a principled way.

1 Introduction

Offline reinforcement learning (RL) greatly increases the range of practical applications of RL to real-world use cases by tackling sequential decision-making through harnessing previously collected datasets of interactions with the environment. For example, offline RL has found application in healthcare [Komorowski et al., 2018, Bachtiger et al., 2020], robotics [Sinha et al., 2022, Kalashnikov et al., 2018, Dasari et al., 2020], autonomous driving [Kendall et al., 2019, Huang et al., 2022] and recommender systems [Xiao and Wang, 2021], scenarios where online data collection with an exploratory policy is either expensive or poses

F. Cuzzolin and M. Sultana (Eds.): Epi UAI 2023, LNAI 14523, pp. 89–100, 2024.
https://doi.org/10.1007/978-3-031-57963-9_7

unacceptable safety risks. However, the absence of online interaction in offline RL amplifies the impact of distributional shift between training and learned policy state-actions, as the agent cannot verify and adjust its beliefs through environment rollouts. Consequently, the agent may mistakenly rely on unsupported actions with high values, unable to correct its belief and lead to very poor policies [Kumar et al., 2019].

Tackling the effects of this distributional shift has been a key focus of offline RL research. A common approach is to explicitly regularise the learned policy to be similar to (or in the support of) the dataset policy [Fujimoto and Gu, 2021, Matsushima et al., 2021, Fujimoto et al., 2019, Kostrikov et al., 2021]. These methods, however, rely on the available data having a significant proportion of high quality demonstrations for the task considered. Some methods entirely avoid off-policy evaluation by carrying out on-policy one-step improvements [Brandfonbrener et al., 2021, Kostrikov et al., 2022] but carry the same conceptual drawback.

Assigning higher values only to supported policies can also be accomplished without artificially constraining the learned policy through alternative forms of regularisation. For example, [Kumar et al., 2020] train a value function regularised so that it forms a conservative estimate of the true value function, but this approach can be overly conservative [Fujimoto and Gu, 2021]. In contrast, uncertainty-based methods only penalise the inferred values for those state-actions that are deemed to have high uncertainty: they come in model-based [Kidambi et al., 2020, Yu et al., 2020] as well as model-free variants such as ensembles of critics [An et al., 2021] or lower confidence bound visitation-based estimates [Shi et al., 2022]. While these methods demonstrate strong empirical performance, they rely on heuristic uncertainty measures and their effectiveness strongly depends on additional hyperparameters (e.g. ensemble size, uncertainty penalty magnitude). Furthermore, while ensembles perform well in quantifying uncertainty in supervised learning [Lakshminarayanan et al., 2017, Ovadia et al., 2019] it is unclear if this carries through to the RL case. More generally, due to the complications that arise from the lack of a ground-truth target, principled uncertainty quantification for model-free RL has been the topic of debate as it is also of interest in online RL [Osband et al., 2018, Touati et al., 2020].

In this work, we propose a principled approach to address the challenges of offline RL by incorporating conservatism, or equivalently pessimism, in the value function prior. We do this by imposing a value prior for any given policy with mean corresponding to the performance of a 'bad' policy (for example, zero-mean in positive reward scenarios). This ensures that during policy evaluation, actions with high posterior values are only those supported by the data, allowing inference to regularize unsupported state-action values without introducing additional uncertainty penalties. As a byproduct of our inference scheme, we are also able to carry out consistent model-free off-policy uncertainty quantification. We empirically demonstrate the effectiveness of this approach using a Gaussian process (GP) critic in the exact inference setting applied to a toy example. We also discuss the current limitations of our framework and future directions for improved scalability. In summary, our main contributions are a method for Bayesian model-free non-episodic off-policy evaluation with uncertainty quantification and a proof of concept that inference with suitably chosen priors is a sufficient ingredient to identify supported policies and is a principled way to tackle distribution shift in offline RL.

2   Preliminaries

We formulate the problem setting in terms of finding a policy that maximises the accumulated discounted reward of a Markov Decision Process (MDP). An MDP is defined as a tuple $(\mathcal{S}, \mathcal{A}, P, \mathcal{R}, \gamma, \rho_0)$ with $\mathcal{S}$ and $\mathcal{A}$ being the state- and action-spaces respectively, P being the transition kernel and $\mathcal{R}$ the state-action dependent (potentially stochastic) reward function. $\gamma \in (0, 1]$ is a discount factor and ρ_0 an initial state distribution, so that the objective is to find a policy π that maximises the expected return $\mathbb{E}(\sum_{t \geq 0} \gamma^t r^{(t)})$ with $r^{(t)} \sim \mathcal{R}(s_t, a_t), s_t \sim P(\cdot|s_{t-1}, a_{t-1}), a_t \sim \pi(\cdot|s_t)$ and $s_0 \sim \rho_0$. In offline RL, the environment's transition dynamics and reward function are unknown and cannot directly be interacted with, but a dataset of observed state, action, reward and next-state transition samples $(s_i, a_i, r_i, s'_i) \in \mathcal{D}$ is available to infer properties of the environment.

Here we focus on environments with deterministic (unknown) transition functions, as it simplifies dynamics inference. We use notation for discrete actions, but the formalism extends analogously to continuous control. We use the shorthand notation of $\mathcal{X}$ to denote the environment's state-action space, so $(s, a) = x \in \mathcal{X} = \mathcal{S} \times \mathcal{A}$. For immediate rewards, we use lower-case r_i to refer to the ith observed reward sample in the dataset and upper-case $R(s_i, a_i)$ or R_i to refer to the (latent) variable representing the mean of the immediate reward's generating process at the ith state-action in the dataset. We will also make the assumption that the mean of the stochastic reward function, and therefore value, is bounded below.

3   Offline RL with Pessimistic Prior

We encode the conservatism necessary in the face of uncertainty by employing a framework that explicitly places a pessimistic prior in function space on the Q-values. As such, the only way for Q-values to be high is if these are directly supported by the observed transitions. We adapt the generative model from Engel et al. [2005], designed for online RL, to the offline case. This involves extending the policy evaluation to be off-policy and non-episodic, while also using Q-values instead of state values for model-free policy improvement.

3.1   Policy Evaluation

The overall strategy is to relate latent (value function) and observed (rewards) variables to carry out direct inference on the latent variables when conditioned on the observations, without requiring iterative value estimation schemes. For any given policy π and transition function $P(s'|s, a)$, Q-values are related to the mean reward R at all state-actions through the Bellman relationship

$$R(s, a) = Q(s, a) - \gamma \sum_{a'} \int ds' \, P(s'|s, a)\pi(a'|s')Q(s', a'). \tag{1}$$

The transition tuples in the dataset $\{(s_i, a_i, r_i, s_i') \in \mathcal{D}\}$ are modelled as being independently generated from a Gaussian distribution with (unknown) mean $R(s_i, a_i)$ and noise σ_r^2. For an environment with a transition function $P(s'|s, a)$ known to be deterministic, the observed reward samples are therefore related to the unknown Q-values through

$$r_i = R(s_i, a_i) + \varepsilon_i$$
$$= Q(s_i, a_i) - \gamma \sum_{a'} \pi(a'|s_i')Q(s_i', a') + \varepsilon_i, \tag{2}$$

with $\varepsilon_i \sim \mathcal{N}(\cdot|0, \sigma_r^2)$ independently sampled.

Since the relationship in Eq. 2 between reward and Q-values at current and next-states is linear, placing a Gaussian prior on Q will also result in a GP and Gaussian prior for R (and therefore r). By placing a (pessimistic) prior directly on Q and determining what the corresponding prior and covariance structure for the policy-dependent linear combination in the right hand side of Eq. 2 is, the resulting GP will capture the correlated nature of the Q-values when the data supports this. For example, if a transition from state s_0 to s_1 results in a reward of 1, assuming negligible noise ε, the posterior joint samples for Q at s_0 and s_1 will result in the Q sample at s_0 taking value 1 greater than the sample at s_1.

Assume an environment with mean reward bounded below. Without loss of generality, take this bound to be 0. We can then introduce a *pessimistic* prior on the Q-values by taking prior mean function equal to 0. Next, we specify a prior covariance function on Q, which we denote as $k_Q : \mathcal{X} \times \mathcal{X} \to \mathbb{R}$. In order to make predictions conditioned on the observed rewards, we must determine the prior covariance of all observed and predicted variables. This requires finding $\text{cov}(r_i, r_j)$ as well as $\text{cov}(Q_k, r_i)$ for $Q_k = Q(x_k)$ at arbitrary state-action pairs.

We start by considering $\text{cov}(R_i, R_j)$ (note $R_i = R(s_i, a_i)$). Let $\hat{\mathcal{X}} = \mathcal{S} \times \mathcal{A} \times \mathcal{S}$. Then, the GP induced on R_i has mean equal to 0 and covariance function $k : \hat{\mathcal{X}} \times \hat{\mathcal{X}} \to \mathbb{R}$ that maps pairs of tuples $\hat{x} = (s, a, s') \in \hat{\mathcal{X}}$ to

$$k(\hat{x}_i, \hat{x}_j) = \sum_{0 \leq k, l \leq n} A_{ik} A_{jl} k_Q(x_i^{(k)}, x_j^{(l)}) \tag{3}$$

for stochastic policies with n discrete actions, where we introduced the notation

$$A_{ij} = \begin{cases} 1 & \text{if } j = 0 \\ -\gamma\pi(a^{(j)}|s_i') & \text{otherwise} \end{cases} \tag{4}$$

$$x_i^{(j)} = \begin{cases} (s_i, a_i) & \text{if } j = 0 \\ (s_i', a^{(j)}) & \text{otherwise} \end{cases} \tag{5}$$

where $a^{(j)}$ denotes the jth of the n actions available. Given the iid. assumption on ε samples, we then have $\text{cov}(r_i, r_j) = \text{cov}(R_i, R_j) + \sigma_r^2\delta_{ij}$. See Appendix 1 for how this prior mean and covariance can be deduced, and note that calculations for $\text{cov}(Q_k, R_i)$ and $\text{cov}(Q_k, Q_{k'})$ can be carried out analogously by choosing different A coefficients. In particular, Q-values Q_k at arbitrary state-actions (or for state-actions that lead to terminal states), correspond to setting $A_{kj} = 1$ if $j = 0$ and 0 otherwise. A proof that this results in a valid positive semi-definite kernel overall if k_Q itself is positive semi-definite is given in Appendix 1.

The posterior mean μ^* and variance Σ^* for the Q-values at arbitrary (s_k, a_k) is then given by the standard Gaussian conditioning expressions [Rasmussen et al., 2006]:

$$\mu^* = \mathbf{K}_{QR}^\top(\mathbf{K}_R + \sigma_r^2\mathbf{I})^{-1}\mathbf{r} \tag{6}$$

$$\Sigma^* = \mathbf{K}_Q - \mathbf{K}_{QR}^\top(\mathbf{K}_R + \sigma_r^2\mathbf{I})^{-1}\mathbf{K}_{QR}, \tag{7}$$

with $\{\mathbf{r}\}_i = r_i$, $\{\mathbf{K}_R\}_{ij} = \text{cov}(R_i, R_j)$, $\{\mathbf{K}_{QR}\}_{ki} = \text{cov}(Q_k, R_i)$ and $\{\mathbf{K}\}_{kk'} = \text{cov}(Q_k, Q_{k'})$. Now, we have a GP that encodes both the pessimism in the face of uncertainty in function space as well as the correct correlations between Q-values samples that ensure consistency with Eq. 2.

3.2   Policy Improvement

The posterior Q-values depend on π at the visited next-states in the dataset. There are a number of possible ways to improve the policy, the most straightforward being to carry out N iterative greedy policy updates so that at each next-state s' visited in the dataset

$$\pi_{n+1}(s') = \text{argmax}_a \, \mathbb{E}_{p(Q(s',a)|\mathcal{D},\pi_n)}Q(s', a). \tag{8}$$

Intuitively, this improves the policy at each next-state according to the posterior Q-values mean given a current policy, so the Q-values of any state-action that lead to this particular next-state will also be improved. At deployment, the rolled-out policy will be, for any arbitrary s,

$$\pi(s) = \text{argmax}_a \, \mathbb{E}_{p(Q(s,a)|\mathcal{D},\pi_N)}Q(s, a). \tag{9}$$

Alternatively, an actor-critic formulation can be employed by considering a parametric (stochastic) actor $\pi_\theta(a|s)$ and optimising the off-policy value objective [Degris et al., 2012]

$$J(\theta) = \sum_{s\in\mathcal{D},a\in\mathcal{A}} \pi_\theta(a|s)\mathbb{E}_{p(Q(s,a)|\mathcal{D},\pi_\theta)}Q(s, a), \tag{10}$$

through gradient ascent steps, as the posterior mean of Q is differentiable with respect to policy parameters. Note that this form optimises value over the state distribution in the dataset, but it may be desirable to marginalise over other state distributions (such as the starting state distribution). The actor's parameters affect this objective both through the probability of taking actions at states s as well as indirectly through the observed next-states $\pi(s')$ in the posterior expectation.

4   Experiments

In this section, we present a toy example to demonstrate the key consequences of our method. Through these experiments, we showcase the following properties of our agent: (1) the ability to piece together transitions from non-episodic datasets and perform 'trajectory stitching' across multiple timesteps to identify supported policies (2) assigning high values to supported policies and low values to out-of-distribution regions of the state space or unsupported state-actions, resulting in (3) learned trajectories that avoid unsupported regions and stay within the in-distribution region, even avoiding actions that are present in the dataset but lead to unsupported regions in subsequent timesteps, and (4) providing a consistent quantification of epistemic uncertainty in the expected return. All of this being a natural byproduct of the inference scheme, with no additional policy constraints or heuristic regularisation.

To highlight these properties, we choose a continuous 2D 'maze' with no walls, a single terminal goal region (with a reward of 1 upon reaching it) and a non-convex region with uniform data density, so that the agent must understand that it should navigate around the region with no data (which is not terminal) for the policy to be correctly supported (see Fig. 1). The actions the agent can take are a step of unit size in any of the 4 cardinal directions and the environment has a discount factor of $\gamma = 0.95$. For each such state, the dataset contains the (s, a, r, s') outcome (including whether s' is terminal) for each of the possible 4 actions.

Figure 1 visualises the maze environment and learned policy at each state present in the dataset. In contrast, we show in Fig. 1b the result of training a naive DQN [Mnih et al., 2015] on the same dataset (with the dataset becoming a fixed replay buffer), where the unmitigated overestimation of Q-values leads to a poorly performing policy. In contrast, Fig. 1c shows the policy and posterior value for the GP critic (with policy improvement as described in Eq. 8) with radial basis function kernel with length-scale 0.25 and unit prior variance: the agent successfully learns to reach the goal while avoiding out-of-distribution regions and assigns high value only to the supported regions. We found that training a parametric actor by optimising objective Eq. 10 converges to similar behaviour. In Fig. 1d we show how the posterior standard deviation of our agent varies throughout state-space, and as is expected is low in the regions where the policy is supported and higher elsewhere. See Appendix 2 for details on hyperparameters and a visualisation of posterior value and standard deviation beyond the main data region.

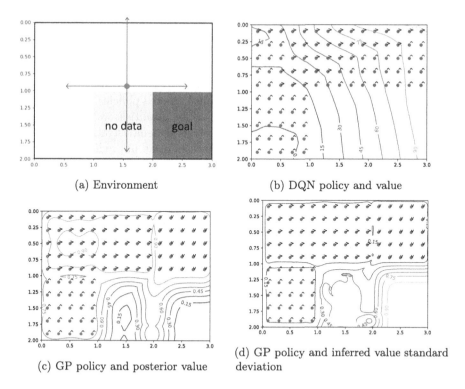

(a) Environment

(b) DQN policy and value

(c) GP policy and posterior value

(d) GP policy and inferred value standard deviation

Fig. 1. The (100) blue dots represent the states in the dataset for which the agent observes transitions after carrying out each action, causing the agent to move by one unit (for a total of 400 transitions), see Fig. 1a. At each state, the learned policy after training is visualised with an arrow symbol ($\wedge, >, \vee, <$ for up, right, down, left respectively) and contours represent the inferred posterior mean (Fig. 1b, 1c) or standard deviation (Fig. 1d) of the value after training. (Color figure online)

5 Conclusion

We have introduced a Bayesian framework to carry out offline, off-policy, model-free policy evaluation for non-episodic datasets that exploits the environment's Markov structure to reason about values across multiple transitions. By encoding pessimism in the prior of the value function and carrying out inference in value function space, we ensure that value after inference is high if and only if it is directly supported by the dataset, making it a suitable critic for offline RL purposes. We implement this in a GP and observe that our method can correctly infer the optimal supported policy for a toy example and assign low values to unsupported policies without requiring heuristic behaviour or value regularisation nor any uncertainty penalties. Our agent is also able to carry out consistent model-free quantification of uncertainty in returns, although it does not require it for decision-making. It is also possible that variants of this setup, such as including optimism in the prior, may find application in online RL for example for guiding exploration.

The main strength of our proposed method is the principled regularisation introduced by inference, ensuring that only policies that lead to out-of-distribution actions are regularised thus avoiding excessive conservatism in the posterior while still assigning low values to unsupported policies. By not requiring behaviour constraints or heuristic uncertainty penalties, we do not require the dataset to contain a large proportion of good demonstrations or for our learned policy to depend on new hyperparameters in an unpredictable way.

On the other hand, the method as presented includes significant limitations. Firstly, the vanilla GP implementation presents scalability challenges, large datasets would require some form of approximate inference [Titsias, 2009, Hensman et al., 2013]. Secondly, some hyperparameters are instead introduced into the prior. While these are arguably easier to interpret and specify, having a hand-crafted functional form for the prior also limits the inherent expressivity of GPs. To address this, an expressive kernel could be learned to tackle high-dimensional problems [Wilson et al., 2016, Ober et al., 2021, van Amersfoort et al., 2021]. While GPs offer a natural way to carry out inference in value-function space, our method is general enough that it may be implemented in other inference frameworks, which may prove easier and more stable to train. For example, a relevant emerging field is that of functional variational inference [Sun et al., 2019, Burt et al., 2020, Ma and Hernández-Lobato, 2021], but other methods that draw connections between inference in function space and other preexisting methods, such as noise contrastive priors [Hafner et al., 2020] or ensembles [D' Angelo and Fortuin, 2021], may be a starting place for including pessimism in the value function prior while still maintaining training stability. Overall, we believe that modelling the conservatism in offline RL as pessimism in the value prior is a principled avenue for improvement of offline RL algorithms.

Acknowledgments. FV was funded by the Department of Computing, Imperial College London. AF was supported by a UKRI Turing AI Fellowship (EP/V025499/1)

Appendix 1

Prior mean and covariance derivation

The prior mean and covariance of the observed rewards can be deduced by writing $R_i = \sum_k A_{ik} Q(x_i^{(k)})$, with the same definition of A and x as given in Eq. 4 and 5 and then considering $\mathbb{E}(R_i)$ and $\text{cov}(R_i, R_j)$.

For the mean, we have

$$\mathbb{E}(R_i) = \mathbb{E} \sum_k A_{ik} Q(x_i^{(k)}) \tag{11}$$

$$= \sum_k A_{ik} \mathbb{E} Q(x_i^{(k)}) \tag{12}$$

$$= 0, \tag{13}$$

and for covariance

$$\text{cov}(R_i, R_j) = \text{cov}\left(\sum_k A_{ik}Q(x_i^{(k)}), \sum_j A_{jl}Q(x_j^{(l)})\right) \tag{14}$$

$$= \sum_{k,l} A_{ik}A_{jl}\text{cov}(Q(x_i^{(k)}), Q(x_j^{(l)})) \tag{15}$$

$$= \sum_{k,l} A_{ik}A_{jl}k_Q(x_i^{(k)}, x_j^{(l)}), \tag{16}$$

as required.

Validity of resulting kernel

To show that k is a valid kernel for any policy, we will deduce that the matrix with elements i, j given by

$$k(\hat{x}_i, \hat{x}_j) = k_{ij} = \sum_{0 \le k,l \le n} A_{ik}A_{jl}k_Q(x_i^{(k)}, x_j^{(l)}) \tag{17}$$

is positive semidefinite (and, trivially, symmetric in i and j) for any given valid kernel k_Q. This is equivalent to the statement that for any vector with elements v_i, the dot product $\sum_{i,j} v_i k_{ij} v_j \ge 0$ given that for any x' and v', $\sum_{m,n} v'_m k_Q(x'_m, x'_n) v'_n \ge 0$.

$$\sum_{i,j} v_i k_{ij} v_j = \sum_{i,j,k,l} v_i A_{ik} v_j A_{jl} k_Q(x_i^{(k)}, x_j^{(l)}) \tag{18}$$

$$= \sum_{(i,j),(k,l)} (v_i A_{ik})(v_j A_{jl})k_Q(x_i^{(k)}, x_j^{(l)}) \tag{19}$$

$$= \sum_{m,n} v'_m v'_n k_Q(x'_m, x'_n) \tag{20}$$

$$\ge 0 \tag{21}$$

as required, where we have 'unrolled' the matrix $v_i A_{ik}$ into the vector v'_m with $x_i^{(k)}$ the corresponding x'_m values and replaced summation over i, k with summation over m and correspondingly summation over j, l with n.

Appendix 2

The GP employed has prior mean equal to 0 and base covariance for the latent (value) variables that factors into an RBF function term in state space and a Kronecker-delta function in action-space (as actions are discrete we assume independence in the value across the different actions) analogously to Engel et al. [2005]:

$$\text{cov}(Q(s_i, a_i), Q(s_j, a_j)) = k_Q((s_i, a_i), (s_j, a_j)) = \sigma_p^2 \exp(\frac{(s_i - s_j)^2}{2l^2})\delta_{a_i a_j}, \quad (22)$$

where we chose $\sigma_p^2 = 1$ and $l = 0.25$ for the experiments presented.

The DQN trained to produce Fig1b has two hidden layers of 256 neurons, batch size 128, Adam optimiser [Kingma and Ba, 2014] with learning rate of 0.001 and was trained for 100k gradient steps.

Here we report the same results from Figs. 1c and 1d but for a wider range of the state-space, where we observe that even outside the main region of interest, in the regions where no data is present the posterior value mean and standard deviation tend to the prior mean and standard deviation, i.e. low value and higher standard deviation, as is desirable in the offline RL setting for unsupported regions.

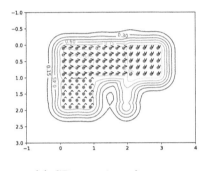
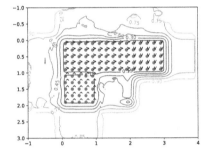

(a) GP posterior value mean   (b) GP posterior value standard deviation

References

An, G., Moon, S., Kim, J.-H., Song, H.O.: Uncertainty-based offline reinforcement learning with diversified q-ensemble. In: Advances in Neural Information Processing Systems, vol. 34, pp. 7436–7447 (2021)

Bachtiger, P., et al.: Artificial intelligence, data sensors and interconnectivity: future opportunities for heart failure. Card. Fail. Rev. **6** (2020)

Brandfonbrener, D., Whitney, W., Ranganath, R., Bruna, J.: Offline RL without off-policy evaluation. In: Advances in Neural Information Processing Systems, vol. 34, pp. 4933–4946 (2021)

Burt, D.R., Ober, S.W., Garriga-Alonso, A., van der Wilk, M.: Understanding variational inference in function-space. arXiv preprint: arXiv:2011.09421 (2020)

Dasari, S., et al.: RoboNet: Large-scale multi-robot learning. In: Conference on Robot Learning, pp. 885–897. PMLR (2020)

Degris, T., White, M., Sutton, R.S.: Off-policy actor-critic. In: Proceedings of the 29th International Conference on Machine Learning, ICML 2012 (2012)

D'Angelo, F., Fortuin, V.: Repulsive deep ensembles are Bayesian. In: Ranzato, M., Beygelzimer, A., Dauphin, Y., Liang, P., Vaughan, J.W. (eds.) Advances in Neural Information Processing Systems, vol. 34, pp. 3451–3465. Curran Associates, Inc. (2021)

Engel, Y., Mannor, S., Meir, R.: Reinforcement learning with Gaussian processes. In: Proceedings of the 22nd International Conference on Machine Learning, pp. 201–208 (2005)

Fujimoto, S., Gu, S.S.: A minimalist approach to offline reinforcement learning. In: Advances in Neural Information Processing Systems, vol. 34, pp. 20132–20145 (2021)

Fujimoto, S., Meger, D., Precup, D.: Off-policy deep reinforcement learning without exploration. In: International Conference on Machine Learning, pp. 2052–2062. PMLR (2019)

Hafner, D., Tran, D., Lillicrap, T., Irpan, A., Davidson, J.: Noise contrastive priors for functional uncertainty. In: Uncertainty in Artificial Intelligence, pp. 905–914. PMLR (2020)

Hensman, J., Fusi, N., Lawrence, N.D.: Gaussian processes for big data. arXiv preprint: arXiv:1309.6835 (2013)

Huang, Z., Wu, J., Lv, C.: Efficient deep reinforcement learning with imitative expert priors for autonomous driving. IEEE Trans. Neural Netw. Learn. Syst. (2022)

Kalashnikov, D., et al.: Scalable deep reinforcement learning for vision-based robotic manipulation. In: Conference on Robot Learning, pp. 651–673. PMLR (2018)

Kendall, A., et a.: Learning to drive in a day. In: 2019 International Conference on Robotics and Automation (ICRA), pp. 8248–8254. IEEE (2019)

Kidambi, R., Rajeswaran, A., Netrapalli, P., Joachims, T.: MOReL: model-based offline reinforcement learning. In: Advances in Neural Information Processing Systems, vol. 33, pp. 21810–21823 (2020)

Kingma, D.P., Ba, J.: Adam: a method for stochastic optimization. arXiv preprint: arXiv:1412.6980 (2014)

Komorowski, M., Celi, L.A., Badawi, O., Gordon, A.C., Faisal, A.A.: The artificial intelligence clinician learns optimal treatment strategies for sepsis in intensive care. Nat. Med. **24**(11), 1716–1720 (2018)

Kostrikov, I., Fergus, R., Tompson, J., Nachum, O.: Offline reinforcement learning with fisher divergence critic regularization. In: International Conference on Machine Learning, pp. 5774–5783. PMLR (2021)

Kostrikov, I., Nair, A., Levine, S.: Offline reinforcement learning with implicit Q-learning. In: International Conference on Learning Representations (2022)

Kumar, A., Fu, J., Soh, M., Tucker, G., Levine, S.: Stabilizing off-policy Q-learning via bootstrapping error reduction. In: Advances in Neural Information Processing Systems, vol. 32 (2019)

Kumar, A., Zhou, A., Tucker, G., Levine, S.: Conservative q-learning for offline reinforcement learning. In: Advances in Neural Information Processing Systems, vol. 33, pp. 1179–1191 (2020)

Lakshminarayanan, B., Pritzel, A., Blundell, C.: Simple and scalable predictive uncertainty estimation using deep ensembles. In: Advances in Neural Information Processing Systems, vol. 30 (2017)

Ma, C., Hernández-Lobato, J.M.: Functional variational inference based on stochastic process generators. In: Advances in Neural Information Processing Systems, vol. 34, pp. 21795–21807 (2021)

Matsushima, T., Furuta, H., Matsuo, Y., Nachum, O., Gu, S.: Deployment-efficient reinforcement learning via model-based offline optimization. In: 9th International Conference on Learning Representations, ICLR 2021, Virtual Event, Austria, May 3-7, 2021. OpenReview.net (2021)

Mnih, V., et al.: Human-level control through deep reinforcement learning. Nature **518**(7540), 529–533 (2015)

Ober, S.W., Rasmussen, C.E., van der Wilk, M.: The promises and pitfalls of deep kernel learning. In: Uncertainty in Artificial Intelligence, pp. 1206–1216. PMLR (2021)

Osband, I., Aslanides, J., Cassirer, A.: Randomized prior functions for deep reinforcement learning. In: Advances in Neural Information Processing Systems, vol. 31 (2018)

Ovadia, Y., et al.: Can you trust your model's uncertainty? evaluating predictive uncertainty under dataset shift. In: Advances in Neural Information Processing Systems, vol. 32, (2019)

Rasmussen, C.E., et al.: Gaussian Processes for Machine Learning, vol. 1. Springer, Cham (2006)

Shi, L., Li, G., Wei, Y., Chen, Y., Chi, Y.: Pessimistic Q-learning for offline reinforcement learning: towards optimal sample complexity. In: International Conference on Machine Learning, pp. 19967–20025. PMLR (2022)

Sinha, S., Mandlekar, A., Garg, A.: S4rl: surprisingly simple self-supervision for offline reinforcement learning in robotics. In: Conference on Robot Learning, pp. 907–917. PMLR (2022)

Sun, S., Zhang, G., Shi, J., Grosse, R.: Functional variational Bayesian neural networks. arXiv preprint: arXiv:1903.05779 (2019)

Titsias, M.: Variational learning of inducing variables in sparse Gaussian processes. In: Artificial Intelligence and Statistics, pp. 567–574. PMLR (2009)

Touati, A., Satija, H., Romoff, J., Pineau, J., Vincent, P.: Randomized value functions via multiplicative normalizing flows. In: Uncertainty in Artificial Intelligence, pp. 422–432. PMLR (2020)

Van Amersfoort, J., Smith, L., Jesson, A., Key, O., Gal, Y.: On feature collapse and deep kernel learning for single forward pass uncertainty. arXiv preprint: arXiv:2102.11409 (2021)

Wilson, A.G., Hu, Z., Salakhutdinov, R., Xing, E.P.: Deep kernel learning. In: Artificial Intelligence and Statistics, pp. 370–378. PMLR (2016)

Xiao, T., Wang, D.: A general offline reinforcement learning framework for interactive recommendation. In: Proceedings of the AAAI Conference on Artificial Intelligence, vol. 35, pp. 4512–4520 (2021)

Yu, T., et al.: MOPO: model-based offline policy optimization. In: Advances in Neural Information Processing Systems, vol. 33, pp. 14129–14142 (2020)

Semantic Attribution for Explainable Uncertainty Quantification

Hanjing Wang[1]([envelope]), Shiqiang Wang[2], and Qiang Ji[3]

[1] Rensselaer Polytechnic Institute, Troy, NY, USA
wangh36@rpi.edu
[2] IBM Thomas J. Watson Research Center, Yorktown Heights, NY, USA
wangshiq@us.ibm.com
[3] Rensselaer Polytechnic Institute, Troy, NY, USA
jiq@rpi.edu

Abstract. Bayesian deep learning, with an emphasis on uncertainty quantification, is receiving growing interest in building reliable models. Nonetheless, interpreting and explaining the origins and reasons for uncertainty presents a significant challenge. In this paper, we present semantic uncertainty attribution as a tool for pinpointing the primary factors contributing to uncertainty. This approach allows us to explain why a particular image carries high uncertainty, thereby making our models more interpretable. Specifically, we utilize the variational autoencoder to disentangle different semantic factors within the latent space and link the uncertainty to corresponding semantic factors for an explanation. The proposed techniques can also enhance explainable out-of-distribution (OOD) detection. We can not only identify OOD samples via their uncertainty, but also provide reasoning rooted in a semantic concept.

Keywords: Bayesian Deep Learning · Uncertainty Attribution

1 Introduction

While conventional deep learning has made remarkable strides in various domains, it is not without its shortcomings. One notable limitation is the inability of these models to effectively quantify the uncertainties associated with their predictions. This can lead to overconfidence in unfamiliar territories, making the models ill-equipped to identify attacks stemming from data perturbations and out-of-distribution inputs.

Predictive uncertainty can be categorized into two distinct types: epistemic uncertainty and aleatoric uncertainty. Epistemic uncertainty arises due to the model's limited understanding of the input, often stemming from a lack of sufficient training data. Aleatoric uncertainty represents the inherent randomness or noise present within the data itself.

Bayesian deep learning (BDL) models present a well-founded framework for estimating the two types of uncertainties. In contrast to conventional point-estimated models, BDL models emphasize the construction of the posterior distribution of model parameters. By generating predictions from a diverse set of

F. Cuzzolin and M. Sultana (Eds.): Epi UAI 2023, LNAI 14523, pp. 101–112, 2024.
https://doi.org/10.1007/978-3-031-57963-9_8

models obtained through sampling the parameter posterior, BDL enables the systematic quantification of predictive uncertainties, providing a more comprehensive understanding of the model's performance and confidence in various situations.

While present BDL methods concentrate on enhancing the accuracy and efficiency of uncertainty quantification (UQ), these approaches are often treated as "black boxes" with limited explainability. Uncertainty attribution (UA) is an essential aspect of UQ that focuses on understanding and explaining the sources and causes of uncertainty within a predictive model. This process offers valuable insights into the model's behavior and allows for enhanced interpretability, trustworthiness, and decision-making in BDL models.

The majority of recently suggested UA methods offer a localized explanation for images that possess high uncertainty. These techniques, often known as local uncertainty attribution strategies, seek to localize the predicted uncertainty by generating an uncertainty map of the input data. This map helps identify the most problematic regions that contribute significantly to prediction uncertainty. By evaluating the contribution of each pixel or data point to the uncertainty, the transparency of BDL models can be substantially improved.

However, local uncertainty attribution falls short in certain scenarios. For instance, when image uncertainty stems from low resolution or random noise, it's impossible to isolate it to a specific region, as these imperfections pervade the whole image. Hence, we propose "semantic uncertainty attribution" for uncertainty reasoning, aiming at identifying the primary factors responsible for input data imperfections that contribute to predictive uncertainty. This method is especially useful in detecting uncertainty sources when data disturbances affect an entire image. Data imperfection mainly arises from data perturbation, indicating noise levels, and data anomaly, reflecting input deviation from the training data distribution. Aleatoric uncertainty basically gauges input perturbations, while epistemic uncertainty measures input anomalies. Nonetheless, image data imperfections can stem from noise, resolution, lighting, object positioning, camera parameters, etc. A deeper understanding of uncertainty sources is desirable, encompassing various types of input perturbations and input anomalies.

In brief, we introduce semantic uncertainty attribution as a method for rationalizing the origins of uncertainty within semantic concepts. Initially, we identify and disentangle the pertinent task-specific factors using a variational autoencoder. Following this, we associate the estimated uncertainty derived from the BDL models with the latent semantic factors to enhance interpretability.

2   Related Work

Classification Attribution. Previous attribution methods have been predominantly developed for classification attribution (CA) using deterministic neural networks to determine the contribution of image pixels to the classification score.

Existing CA methods can be broadly categorized into two groups: gradient-based methods and perturbation-based methods. Gradient-based methods [8, 19–23, 25, 27] leverage gradient information as input attribution, providing insights into the relationship between input features and model predictions. For example, [21] employed the raw gradient to compute the importance of features. To smooth out these raw gradients, [20] multiplied the gradients with the inputs. [22] combined the gradients from several noisy inputs, while [23] accumulated the gradients through a path integral from a reference input to the target input. Perturbation-based methods [3, 5, 6, 15, 17, 26] offer an alternative approach to attributing the contributions of different features by modifying the input and observing the subsequent changes in the model's output.

Local Uncertainty Attribution. As shown by [24], CA methods may not be reliable when applied directly to localize uncertainty for identifying problematic regions in the input data. However, various CA methods can be adapted for local uncertainty attribution. Gradient-based CA methods can be extended for uncertainty attribution by adjusting their focus from the model output to the uncertainty. In this paper, we extend gradient [21], Input-G [20], Smooth-Grad [22], and IG [23] for UA. Likewise, perturbation-based methods can also be applied to uncertainty localization by observing the changes in uncertainty corresponding to input alterations. In recent years, several methods have been specifically designed for UA. For instance, CLUE [1] and its variants [11, 12] focus on creating an improved image with minimal uncertainty by modifying the uncertain input using a generative model. The attribution map is generated by measuring the difference between the original input and the modified input. To further enhance pixel-wise attributions, [14] combined the CLUE method with the path integral technique. To relax the assumptions of the generative model, [24] proposed UA-Backprop for attributing the input within a single backward pass.

Semantic Uncertainty Attribution. Studies for identifying key factors causing high uncertainty in the input data are limited. This complex field necessitates a deep understanding of the data generation process to isolate intertwined factors during learning. [16] attempted to identify uncertainty sources in image object classification by building a variational autoencoder (VAE) with disentangled latent representations. They developed a classification model to predict labels directly from these disentangled representations, computing each factor's attribution score from its optimized uncertainty reduction. However, this field is still under-researched. The applicability of unsupervised disentangled learning for uncertainty attribution remains uncertain. The framework's dual use of features for reconstruction and classification may impair the latter. It also requires solving computation-intensive multi-optimization problems, highlighting a need for more efficient methods. Evaluations of uncertainty attribution methods must also be carefully designed due to the absent ground truth reasoning.

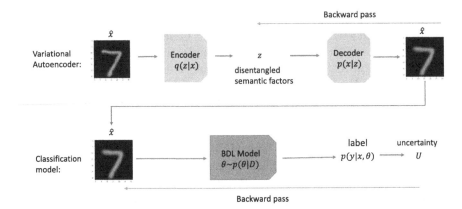

Fig. 1. The overall process of the semantic uncertainty attribution. The blue lines represent the forward propagation and the orange lines represent the backward propagation. (Color figure online)

3   Proposed Methods

3.1   Overall Framework

In this study, we present a unique framework using a pre-trained VAE to interpret uncertainty produced by a BDL model. This requires two pre-trained models: a disentangled VAE and a BDL model for classification. The VAE encodes inputs into a disentangled latent space, where each latent factor symbolizes a specific semantic factor. We utilize a Bayesian classification model since it can explain both aleatoric and epistemic uncertainties. Differing from [16], the VAE and the classification model are trained independently to preserve their performance. The attribution process is reserved only for images with high uncertainty.

During the uncertainty reasoning process, our initial step is to link the pre-trained VAE with the classification model for a combined attribution effort. To accomplish this, we feed the image into the VAE for reconstruction. Subsequently, the reconstructed image serves as the input for the classification model to estimate uncertainty. Notably, this approach allows the estimated uncertainty to be a function of the disentangled latent factors, thereby enabling a backward computation of each semantic factor's contribution to the uncertainty. An overall framework is shown in Fig. 1 and more details are elaborated in the subsequent sections.

3.2   Disentangled VAE

To identify the essential factors, we propose leveraging recent advancements in disentangled representation learning [2,7,9,13,18]. We aim to construct a variational autoencoder with an encoder $q(z|x)$ and a decoder $p(x|z)$ to learn interpretable latent representations $z = [z_1, z_2, \cdots, z_K]^T$ that correspond to perturbation factors. The learning of these latent representations varies, which depends on the level of supervision provided. In the initial phase, our assumption is that there is no supervision for the semantic factors and we only have access to the classification label for each image.

To learn the interpretable factors, we employ the $\beta-$VAE [7]. The loss function for the $\beta-$VAE of a single input x is presented as follows:

$$L(x) = -\mathbb{E}_{z\sim q(z|x)}[\log p(x|z)] + \beta D_{KL}(q(z|x)||p(z)) \tag{1}$$

where D_{KL} represents the Kullback-Leibler (KL) divergence and $p(z) = \mathcal{N}(0, I)$ is designated as a standard Gaussian distribution, which acts as the prior distribution for z. The hyperparameter β, which is greater than 1, is utilized to create a balance between the reconstruction performance and the capacity for disentanglement. In the case of a standard VAE, β is equal to 1. However, it has been demonstrated that a larger β value can enhance the performance of disentanglement. It's important to underscore that, in the absence of supervision, we cannot guarantee the disentanglement of all relevant factors. However, when data are methodically generated from diverse factors, we can strive to disentangle these factors to the best of our ability using those unsupervised methods. Besides $\beta-$VAE, other methods can also be employed such as [2,13,18]. The performance of attribution is reliant on the disentangled factors, and we cannot assign attribution to a factor that the VAE has not recognized. Within the framework of unsupervised disentangled representation learning, we can discern the meaning of each factor by visualizing an image trajectory.

In our forthcoming research, we plan to disentangle the factors of interest by leveraging various degrees of supervision. When strong supervision is accessible, which implies we have knowledge of these factors' values, we can develop a model that maps the inputs to their corresponding factors. In cases where weak supervision is provided, such as inputs being grouped by similar semantic factors except for one distinct factor, without knowing the specific values of the factors, we can use weakly-supervised disentangled representation learning methods like the one proposed by [9]. In most cases, self-supervision combined with standard data augmentation techniques proves sufficient for disentangling numerous factors essential for classification such as resolution, illumination, rotation, color, and random Gaussian noise.

3.3   Classification Model

In this study, we utilize the deep ensemble method [10] for classification[1], enabling calculating both aleatoric and epistemic uncertainties. Basically, N models parameterized by $\{\theta_s\}_{s=1}^{S}$ are trained independently with different initializations, donated as $p(y|x, \theta_i)$. In the context of classification tasks, entropy can be used to assess the uncertainty in class predictions [4]:

$$\underbrace{\mathcal{H}\left[\mathrm{p}(y|x, \mathcal{D})\right]}_{\text{Total Uncertainty}} = \underbrace{\mathcal{I}\left[y, \theta|x, \mathcal{D}\right]}_{\text{Epistemic Uncertainty}} + \underbrace{\mathbb{E}_{\mathrm{p}(\theta|\mathcal{D})}\left[\mathcal{H}[\mathrm{p}(y|x, \theta)]\right]}_{\text{Aleatoric Uncertainty}} \tag{2}$$

---

[1] There is debate over whether deep ensemble is a Bayesian method. We believe it is since each ensemble component can serve as a mode of $p(\theta|\mathcal{D})$.

where $\mathcal{H}$ and $\mathcal{I}$ represent the entropy and mutual information, respectively. $\mathcal{D}$ is the training data and $p(\theta|\mathcal{D})$ is the posterior distribution of parameters. More specifically,

$$
\mathcal{H}\left[p(y|x,\mathcal{D})\right] = \mathcal{H}\left[E_{p(\theta|\mathcal{D})}[p(y|x,\theta)]\right] \approx \mathcal{H}\left[\frac{1}{S}\sum_{s=1}^{S}p(y|x,\theta^s)\right].
$$
$$
\mathbb{E}_{p(\theta|\mathcal{D})}\left[\mathcal{H}[p(y|x,\theta)]\right] \approx \frac{1}{S}\sum_{s=1}^{S}\mathcal{H}(p(y|x,\theta^s)).
$$
(3)

3.4   Semantic Uncertainty Attribution

Forward Propagation. With a pre-trained VAE and the classification model at hand, the process initiates with forward propagation, where high-uncertain images are first fed into the VAE. The VAE's encoder produces the mean and covariance matrix of the latent representation z. The mean from the distribution of z is then used as the input for the decoder to generate a reconstructed image. Following this, the reconstructed image is inputted into the BDL model for estimating uncertainty. It's important to highlight that the proposed method is applicable to any form of uncertainty as defined in Eq. (2).

Backward Propagation. Rather than resorting to a simplistic attribution method, we exploit the current advancements in explainable AI techniques for effective and precise UA. We incorporate some gradient-based CA techniques and adapt them for UA purposes. Our findings indicate that several methods perform quite satisfactorily, eliminating the need to formulate a specific algorithm exclusively for semantic UA. For the backpropagation step, we test several approaches, restricting our focus only to gradient-based methods to ensure optimal efficiency.

SemanticUA-G: In this approach, we utilize the absolute values of the raw gradients from uncertainty U to the latent representation z as the attribution scores. These scores are represented by Eq. (4):

$$
A_G(z) = \left|\frac{\partial U}{\partial z}\right|.
$$
(4)

In this section, the latent variable z refers to the mean value of the distribution generated by the VAE encoder. The vector $A(z) = [A(z_1), A(z_2), \cdots, A(z_N)]^T$ matches the size of z. Each element, $A(z_i)$, represents the contribution of the ith factor to the overall uncertainty.

SemanticUA-InputG: To account for the potential noise in the raw gradients, an alternative approach is to utilize the InputG method [20]:

$$
A_{InputG}(z) = \left|z \odot \frac{\partial U}{\partial z}\right|.
$$
(5)

where $\odot$ represents the element-wise product.

SemanticUA-SG: SmoothGrad [22] aims to reduce the impact of noisy gradients by aggregating attributions from multiple noisy inputs. Let's denote T as the number of noisy images created by adding Gaussian noise. These noisy images are fed into the encoder, resulting in T noisy latent representations denoted as $\{z^{(t)}\}_{t=1}^{T}$. The computation of $z^{(t)}$ involves applying the function $E_z[q(z|x+\epsilon^{(t)}))]$, where $\epsilon^{(t)} \sim \mathcal{N}(0,\sigma^2 I)$ is a random noise sampled from a Gaussian distribution with a mean of 0 and covariance matrix $\sigma^2 I$. Here, σ represents a hyperparameter and I denotes the identity matrix. Finally, the attribution score is generated using Eq. (6):

$$A_{SG}(z) = \frac{1}{T}\sum_{t=1}^{T} A_G(z^{(t)}).\tag{6}$$

SemanticUA-IG: We can utilize the integrated gradient (IG) [23] method for uncertainty attribution. The adapted version of this method for UA establishes a path integral from a reference latent representation z_0 to z, accumulating the uncertainty gradients U with respect to the latent representations on the path from z_0 to z, as demonstrated in Eq. (7):

$$A_{IG}(z) = (z - z_0) \odot \int_0^1 \frac{\partial U(z_0 + \alpha(z - z_0))}{\partial z}d\alpha.\tag{7}$$

Given that the reference input z_0 bears no uncertainty, the property of completeness is fulfilled, ensuring that the sum of the attribution scores equates to the uncertainty itself:

$$U = \sum_i A_{IG}(z_i).\tag{8}$$

Since IG requires a reference input z_0, we randomly choose z_0 by the encoding of an image from the training data with low uncertainty.

4   Experiment

Dataset. We employ the colored MNIST dataset for image classification and the disentanglement of semantic factors. As part of our future work, we plan to extend our analysis to include more datasets.

Disentangled VAE. To achieve the disentanglement of semantic factors, we employ β-VAE, an unsupervised approach. We can visualize the meaning of each factor through an image trajectory. The implementation code, utilizing the default model architecture and hyperparameters, can be found at the following URL: https://github.com/YannDubs/disentangling-vae.

Bayesian Deep Learning Model. For approximating the posterior distribution of parameters and performing uncertainty quantification, we utilize the deep ensemble method [10]. This approach involves training five ensemble models independently, each initialized differently. We employ the following architecture: Conv2D-Relu-Dropout-Conv2D-Relu-MaxPool2D-Dropout-Dense-Relu-Dropout-Dense-Softmax. Each convolutional layer consists of 32 convolution filters with a kernel size of 4×4. Additionally, we utilize a max-pooling layer with a kernel size of 2×2, two dense layers with 128 units, and a dropout probability of 0.25. The batch size is set to 128, and the maximum epoch is 50. We employ the SGD optimizer with a learning rate of 0.01, a momentum of 0.9, and a weight decay of 0.0005.

Baselines. We introduce several attribution methods, namely SemanticUA-G, SemanticUA-InputG, SemanticUA-SG, and SemanticUA-IG, by employing different techniques. For SemanticUA-IG, we approximate the integration in Eq. (7) by sample average, where 200 samples of α are linearly generated between 0 and 1. For SemanticUA-SG, the number of noisy images, denoted as T, is equal to 200. The added noise is sampled from a Gaussian distribution with 0 mean and 0.1 standard deviation. Due to the relatively limited exploration in this area, we conduct a comparison of our method exclusively with SourceUA [16].

4.1   Explainable OOD Detection

In this experiment, our objective is to detect synthetically generated out-of-distribution samples and provide explanations for why they differ from the training data. The experiment is structured in a way that we have prior knowledge of the underlying reasons for problematic images. We then assess the capability of our approaches to identify these reasons through the utilization of the backpropagation step.

Experiment Setting. For training the disentangled VAE, we employ the colored MNIST dataset, which allows us to disentangle a specific factor representing the digit's color. Figure 2 illustrates that z_5 corresponds to the color factor of the digit. In this experiment, we train the classification model exclusively on red images. Consequently, when encountering images with green or blue colors, the BDL classification model should exhibit large uncertainty. Thus, we can conclude that the primary factor contributing to the observed predictive uncertainty is the color itself. Subsequently, we apply our semantic UA method to identify the reasons behind the high uncertainty observed in images with different colors. We utilize total uncertainty for this evaluation.

Evaluation Metric. We design the accuracy (ACC) by the percentage of the number of successes in the detection of the color factor that contributes most to the uncertainty. Let $\{z^m\}_{m=1}^M$ denote the encodings of the testing images. The detection accuracy can be calculated in the following equation:

$$ACC = \frac{1}{M} \sum_{m=1}^{M} \delta(\arg \max_{k=1:K} A(z_k^m) = 5) \tag{9}$$

image trajectory

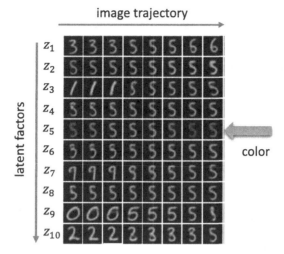

Fig. 2. The image trajectory for the disentangled VAE. Each row represents the image trajectory for a particular semantic factor. The reconstructed images are displayed by smoothly transitioning the values of z_k from small to large while keeping the other latent factors fixed.

where δ is a delta function that returns 1 only when $\arg\max_{k=1:K} A(z_k^m) = 5$ and otherwise, it will return 0. Our objective is not only to ensure that the "color" latent factor is the primary source of uncertainty but also to ensure that it is the sole source of uncertainty. This is because, during the generation of problematic images, we solely modify the color information. As a result, we anticipate that the color factor can account for nearly 100% of the uncertainty. The explanation rate for factor z_k can be defined as follows:

$$ER(k) = \frac{1}{M} \sum_{m=1}^{M} \frac{\exp(A(z_k^m))}{\sum_{j=1}^{K} \exp(A(z_j^m))}. \tag{10}$$

In our experiment, our expectation is that $ER(5)$, the explanation rate for the color factor, should be maximized for images with different colors in comparison to the training data.

Experiment Results. The results presented in Table 1 demonstrate the substantial improvement achieved by our semantic uncertainty attribution framework compared to SourceUA. This improvement can primarily be attributed to the fact that SourceUA directly utilizes disentangled latent representations from the VAE as input to the classifier, which can negatively impact the accuracy of uncertainty quantification in the classification model. Among the various methods within our framework, SemanticUA-IG stands out with the highest performance. It achieves nearly 100% accuracy in identifying the underlying causes of uncertainty when provided with ground truth information.

Table 1. ACC, ER(5), and empirical runtime for semantic UA evaluation on colored MNIST dataset. The last column displays the time required to attribute a single input. In the case of green and blue images, where the color factor primarily drives uncertainty, we anticipate a higher value for ACC and ER(5). Conversely, for red images, we expect lower values for ACC and ER(5) because color is not the primary source of predictive uncertainty in this context.

Method	Green		Blue		Red		UA Time
	ACC ↑	ER(5) ↑	ACC ↑	ER(5) ↑	ACC ↓	ER(5) ↓	
SemanticUA-G	0.733	0.220	0.523	0.139	0.013	**0.095**	0.04 s
SemanticUA-InputG	0.450	0.137	0.400	0.122	0.107	0.096	0.04 s
SemanticUA-SG	0.623	0.257	0.467	0.118	**0.000**	0.096	0.65 s
SemanticUA-IG	**1.000**	**0.503**	**0.987**	**0.448**	**0.000**	0.100	0.66 s
SourceUA	0.050	0.101	0.057	0.102	0.027	0.101	28.44 s

5 Conclusion

In conclusion, this paper has explored the application of semantic uncertainty attribution in the context of Bayesian deep learning, with a particular focus on uncertainty quantification and interpretation. By leveraging the variational autoencoder, we successfully disentangled various semantic factors within the latent space, enabling us to attribute uncertainty to specific factors. This approach significantly enhances the interpretability of our models by providing explanations for high uncertainty in individual images. Moreover, we have demonstrated the utility of these techniques in improving OOD detection, where not only can we identify OOD samples based on their uncertainty, but we can also offer explanations grounded in semantic concepts.

In our future work, we plan to expand our disentanglement efforts to encompass additional classification-relevant factors such as image resolution, illumination, and random noise. We will explore various disentangled representation learning methods to effectively disentangle and attribute these factors to different types of uncertainty, thereby enhancing our understanding of the distinctions between aleatoric and epistemic uncertainty. Furthermore, we aim to leverage the estimated semantic uncertainty attribution to improve model performance, taking a step beyond mere explanation toward the development of actionable Bayesian deep learning techniques. By incorporating these advancements, we can construct models that not only provide explanations but also actively utilize uncertainty information to drive improved performance and decision-making.

References

1. Antorán, J., Bhatt, U., Adel, T., Weller, A., Hernández-Lobato, J.M.: Getting a clue: A method for explaining uncertainty estimates. arXiv preprint: arXiv:2006.06848 (2020)

2. Chen, R.T., Li, X., Grosse, R.B., Duvenaud, D.K.: Isolating sources of disentangle-ment in variational autoencoders. In: Advances in Neural Information Processing Systems, vol. 31 (2018)

3. Dabkowski, P., Gal, Y.: Real time image saliency for black box classifiers. In: Advances in Neural Information Processing Systems, vol. 30 (2017)

4. Depeweg, S., Hernandez-Lobato, J.M., Doshi-Velez, F., Udluft, S.: Decomposition of uncertainty in bayesian deep learning for efficient and risk-sensitive learning. In: International Conference on Machine Learning, pp. 1184–1193. PMLR (2018)

5. Fong, R., Patrick, M., Vedaldi, A.: Understanding deep networks via extremal perturbations and smooth masks. In: Proceedings of the IEEE/CVF International Conference on Computer Vision, pp. 2950–2958 (2019)

6. Fong, R.C., Vedaldi, A.: Interpretable explanations of black boxes by meaningful perturbation. In: Proceedings of the IEEE International Conference on Computer Vision, pp. 3429–3437 (2017)

7. Higgins, I., et al.: beta-VAE: learning basic visual concepts with a constrained variational framework (2016)

8. Kapishnikov, A., Venugopalan, S., Avci, B., Wedin, B., Terry, M., Bolukbasi, T.: Guided integrated gradients: an adaptive path method for removing noise. In: Proceedings of the IEEE/CVF Conference on Computer Vision and Pattern Recognition, pp. 5050–5058 (2021)

9. Kulkarni, T.D., Whitney, W.F., Kohli, P., Tenenbaum, J.: Deep convolutional inverse graphics network. In: Advances in Neural Information Processing Systems, vol. 28 (2015)

10. Lakshminarayanan, B., Pritzel, A., Blundell, C.: Simple and scalable predictive uncertainty estimation using deep ensembles (2016). http://arxiv.org/abs/1612.01474

11. Ley, D., Bhatt, U., Weller, A.: {\delta}-clue: diverse sets of explanations for uncer-tainty estimates. arXiv preprint: arXiv:2104.06323 (2021)

12. Ley, D., Bhatt, U., Weller, A.: Diverse, global and amortised counterfactual expla-nations for uncertainty estimates. In: Proceedings of the AAAI Conference on Artificial Intelligence, vol. 36, pp. 7390–7398 (2022)

13. Margonis, V., Davvetas, A., Klampanos, I.A.: Wela-VAE: learning alternative disentangled representations using weak labels. arXiv preprint: arXiv:2008.09879 (2020)

14. Perez, I., Skalski, P., Barns-Graham, A., Wong, J., Sutton, D.: Attribution of pre-dictive uncertainties in classification models. In: The 38th Conference on Uncer-tainty in Artificial Intelligence (2022)

15. Petsiuk, V., Das, A., Saenko, K.: Rise: Randomized input sampling for explanation of black-box models. arXiv preprint: arXiv:1806.07421 (2018)

16. Rey, L.A.P., İşler, B., Holenderski, M., Jarnikov, D.: Identifying the sources of uncertainty in object classification (2020)

17. Ribeiro, M.T., Singh, S., Guestrin, C.: " why should i trust you?" explaining the predictions of any classifier. In: Proceedings of the 22nd ACM SIGKDD Interna-tional Conference on Knowledge Discovery and Data Mining, pp. 1135–1144 (2016)

18. Sarhan, M.H., Eslami, A., Navab, N., Albarqouni, S.: Learning interpretable disen-tangled representations using adversarial VAEs. In: Wang, Q., et al. (eds.) Domain Adaptation and Representation Transfer and Medical Image Learning with Less Labels and Imperfect Data. Lecture Notes in Computer Science(), vol. 11795, pp. 37–44. Springer, Cham (2019). https://doi.org/10.1007/978-3-030-33391-1_5

19. Selvaraju, R.R., Cogswell, M., Das, A., Vedantam, R., Parikh, D., Batra, D.: Grad-CAM: visual explanations from deep networks via gradient-based localization. In: Proceedings of the IEEE International Conference on Computer Vision, pp. 618–626 (2017)
20. Shrikumar, A., Greenside, P., Shcherbina, A., Kundaje, A.: Not just a black box: learning important features through propagating activation differences. arXiv preprint: arXiv:1605.01713 (2016)
21. Simonyan, K., Vedaldi, A., Zisserman, A.: Deep inside convolutional networks: visualising image classification models and saliency maps. arXiv preprint: arXiv:1312.6034 (2013)
22. Smilkov, D., Thorat, N., Kim, B., Viégas, F., Wattenberg, M.: SmoothGrad: removing noise by adding noise. arXiv preprint: arXiv:1706.03825 (2017)
23. Sundararajan, M., Taly, A., Yan, Q.: Axiomatic attribution for deep networks. In: International Conference on Machine Learning, pp. 3319–3328. PMLR (2017)
24. Wang, H., Joshi, D., Wang, S., Ji, Q.: Gradient-based uncertainty attribution for explainable Bayesian deep learning. In: Proceedings of the IEEE/CVF Conference on Computer Vision and Pattern Recognition, pp. 12044–12053 (2023)
25. Xu, S., Venugopalan, S., Sundararajan, M.: Attribution in scale and space. In: Proceedings of the IEEE/CVF Conference on Computer Vision and Pattern Recognition, pp. 9680–9689 (2020)
26. Yang, Q., Zhu, X., Fwu, J.K., Ye, Y., You, G., Zhu, Y.: MFPP: morphological fragmental perturbation pyramid for black-box model explanations. In: 2020 25th International Conference on Pattern Recognition (ICPR), pp. 1376–1383. IEEE (2021)
27. Zeiler, M.D., Fergus, R.: Visualizing and understanding convolutional networks. In: Fleet, D., Pajdla, T., Schiele, B., Tuytelaars, T. (eds.) Computer Vision - ECCV 2014. Lecture Notes in Computer Science, vol. 8689, pp. 818–833. Springer, Cham (2014). https://doi.org/10.1007/978-3-319-10590-1_53

Author Index

F. Cuzzolin and M. Sultana (Eds.): Epi UAI 2023, LNAI 14523, p. 113, 2024.
https://doi.org/10.1007/978-3-031-57963-9

Printed in the United States
by Baker & Taylor Publisher Services

Printed in the United States
by Baker & Taylor Publisher Services